When You Need to Take a Stand

Resources for Living

Andrew D. Lester
General Editor

When You Need
to Take a Stand

Carolyn Stahl Bohler

Westminster/John Knox Press
Louisville, Kentucky

PJC MILTON CAMPUS LRC

© 1990 Carolyn Stahl Bohler

All rights reserved—no part of this book may be reproduced in any form without permission in writing from the publisher, except by a reviewer who wishes to quote brief passages in connection with a review in magazine or newspaper.

Scripture quotations from the Revised Standard Version of the Bible are copyrighted 1946, 1952, © 1971, 1973 by the Division of Christian Education of the National Council of the Churches of Christ in the U.S.A. and are used by permission.

The quotation in chapter 3 from Meg Gerrard is reprinted from Kathryn Kelley, ed., *Females, Males, and Sexuality,* by permission of the State University of New York Press, copyright © 1987, State University of New York.

The quotation from Martin Luther King, Jr., in chapter 7 is copyright © 1963 by Martin Luther King, Jr., and reprinted by permission of Joan Daves.

Book design by Gene Harris

First edition

Published by Westminster/John Knox Press
Louisville, Kentucky

PRINTED IN THE UNITED STATES OF AMERICA

9 8 7 6 5 4 3 2 1

Library of Congress Cataloging-in-Publication Data

Bohler, Carolyn Stahl, 1948–
    When you need to take a stand / Carolyn Stahl Bohler. — 1st ed.
        p.   cm. — (Resources for living)
    Includes bibliographical references.
    ISBN 0–664–25051–3

    1. Assertiveness (Psychology) 2. Interpersonal conflict.
3. Values—Psychological aspects.   4. Christian life—Methodist
authors.   I. Title.   II. Series.
BF575.A85B63 1990
158′.2—dc20   89–29047
                                                            CIP

92-3086 mcl

Dedicated to John

who hears me into speech

Contents

Acknowledgments

The idea for this book emerged from discussions with Andrew D. Lester; I thank him for the invitation to write about speaking. Several communities responded to ideas presented in this work while the thoughts were in their formative stages: pastors of the West Virginia Annual Conference of the United Methodist Church, a small group of Doctor of Ministry students at United Theological Seminary, the broader United Theological Seminary in Dayton, Ohio, and a workshop at the American Association of Pastoral Counselors' meeting in St. Louis in the spring of 1988. I appreciate the generous responses from these colleagues. Powell S. Hall, a minister in West Virginia, provided enthusiastic help, including making Greek a little less "Greek" to me. Two friends, Bridget Claire McKeever and Penny Matthews, were insightful and supportive. Marti Anderson, our faculty secretary, was helpful in a variety of ways, including the bestowing of encouraging words. I am thankful, too, to Charles Brown, with whom I consulted, for his time and expertise. I appreciate the kind and thoughtful care my sister, Marilyn Collins, took in reading the manuscript.

My husband, John, read every draft and shared much editorial advice. I am grateful for his compassionate support and wisdom.

When You Need to Take a Stand

1

Speaking Up in Relationships

You want to speak up about child rearing, but you don't want your daughter-in-law to be angry with you. You want to speak up at home, but you don't want to hurt your spouse. You want to speak up at work, but you are not sure of your position and don't want to look like a fool. So you act tongue-tied, not speaking up, and you feel frustrated, resentful, or angry.

A couple face a dilemma. Both of them work outside the home, and their child-care arrangements have fallen through. The father's mother, who is sixty-two, has just retired from her work. The father would like to ask his mother if she could provide child care for them on a regular part-time basis. He has not asked her for anything so important for a long time, and he is unsure how to approach her.

A woman has been dating a man for almost six months. She perceives that the relationship is rather good, but she is beginning to boil over each time her friend telephones her in distress, wondering where she has been for the past hour or so. For several months she has dutifully responded with her exact whereabouts whenever her friend inquired. Now she realizes that she cannot stay in the relationship on a committed, long-term basis unless this constant demand to report to him is eliminated; she needs to be trusted to have some independence. She asks herself often how she can talk to him about this problem, fretting over when, if, and how to bring it up.

When something emerges that matters a great deal in a relationship, it often happens that we get stuck asking ourselves whether or not to speak about it. We may be stuck for months, vacillating between "I'll mention it today" and "I don't think it's the right time just yet."

The Judeo-Christian tradition teaches that we need to use wisdom when we speak, but many Jews and Christians internalize only part of the message— namely, "Hold your tongue." We could instead choose to follow the example of the psalmist: "My heart over- flows with a goodly theme; . . . my tongue is like the pen of a ready scribe" (Ps. 45:1).

For centuries people have asked how much to speak and how much silence to keep—when to speak and when to listen. We need to think of this not as two opposite acts but as two parts of a single process. Some- times we think we can function by holding our tongue—it is easier that way. Eventually we realize that holding our thoughts isn't possible in intimate relation- ships.

The attempt to hold back our thoughts is similar to what my daughter experienced when she was trying to swim. It was natural for her to think that she had to begin by *holding* her breath. But when I was swimming laps myself, I realized that if I focused on *holding* my breath I was scared; I felt restricted. If I *gave* my breath to the water, blowing out the air in the water as if I had plenty, I could take a breath when I lifted my head, then give it once again to the water. I could give and take breath freely; I never had to hold it. I explained this to my daughter, and she began practicing blowing out under the water. This enabled her to swim with several strokes and, most important, to befriend the water. She was ready for the next step in learning to swim.

If we were to think of speaking within relationships as giving and receiving breath, we would be more able to relax, to share, to move and speak naturally—as naturally as a swimmer moves and breathes. We could speak, listen, speak, and listen in a rhythm characterized by generosity and sharing. Speaking *is* a gift, just as listening is; it needs to be given and received generously in any important relationship.

When we have difficulty speaking, it's usually because we have a stand we are reluctant to take. A stand—what we want to say—is the coalescing of our values to the point of clarity and action. It is the coming together of our values in a new and clear way.

A student teacher values speaking quietly in the classroom. His supervisor observes him and suggests that sometimes he needs to shout in order to establish his authority. The student teacher thinks about this and realizes how strongly he values being an example and how much he thinks that his being quiet is good for the children. His values have come together clearly, to the point where he develops a stand about his approach to teaching. He is able to say to his supervisor that he is going to try teaching without shouting.

A stand emerges or is made known when our values are challenged, confronted, or attacked. For example, a woman values frankness and sincerity, the lack of secretiveness. Her boss lets her know that one of her co-workers is going to be fired but tells her that she is not to inform that person. At first the woman feels some discomfort at being given that information, but later in the day she realizes more clearly that her boss's confidential remark is a challenge to her values, and she also realizes that she must take a stand. She returns to the boss to say that now that she knows this information, the co-worker needs to know too, for it is not right that someone not know about decisions regarding himself or herself when others do.

Challenges may evoke the awareness of values people did not realize they held so dearly. A family had taken vacations regularly for several years. As one child entered Little League, the family had to decide what to do when the games scheduled overlapped the family vacation time. The family discussed the values they held that were pertinent to this decision: sports and team play for each member, family togetherness, and adventure on vacations. They emerged with a stand, agreed to by the whole family: While they were in town the games would be given a high priority, but when it was time for vacation, the family trips were more important than attending every game.

The challenge that evokes the stand may come from other individuals or from the community. The student teacher was challenged by his supervisor, the worker by her boss, and the family by the Little League schedule. However, simply learning new information can bring forth a stand. A man values caring for the earth in order to pass it on to future generations. He is concerned for the environment and his part in keeping it healthy. When he learns that fluorocarbons present in aerosol cans deplete the ozone layer, causing environmental damage, he takes a stand not to use aerosol cans.

Stand taking is not only brought about with facts about nature and things; learning facts about people is often enough to help us take a very different stand toward them. A man may be impatient with a woman who says that she wants to be a friend but who has a difficult time accepting kind gestures. When the man discovers that she has been widowed twice, though she is just forty-five, he is more understanding of her reluctance to enter into friendships.

Our values may be held without our full awareness of them. For instance, the woman who was told the secret by her boss was not aware that she held sincerity and honesty as such strong values until those values were challenged. Neither did the family realize how much they valued their adventurous trips until they questioned whether they were willing to give them up.

We speak up with actions as well as words. A hug after an argument is a way of speaking forgiveness. Moving over to the passenger's seat to let your teenager drive conveys a coalescing of values to a new position of trust. A haircut and a shave (or growing a beard) are acts that have large symbolic value in many relationships. However, whenever these gestures are made without words attached, the meaning is not always clear. "Did he cut his hair because he knows I like it that way, or for some other reason?"

A "stand" is not a "sit"; it is not something that is undertaken in a laid-back or casual manner. People running for public office may take "positions," but people who are eager to communicate their values stand up; they put themselves forward.

A stand has similarities to a decision, but there is a distinction between the two. They are alike in that both decisions and stands require a mobilizing of internal forces in the direction of action. In contrast, wishing or willing can be done by playfully entertaining ideas without any commitment to action, but decision making and stand taking include the intent to act. We make myriad decisions daily (what to do, to eat, to say); we take far fewer stands.

The distinction between a stand and a decision is that when we take a stand some of our values are on the line, whereas a decision can be made without a confrontation of our values. I decide to go to work, decide to go grocery shopping, decide to attend a parent-teacher organization meeting at my child's school. But when I vote to invite the city's realtors to see the quality of the public schools, I stand for public education.

Obviously, a decision is implicit in every stand. We decide to stand; we decide to speak. The reverse is not true—we do not need to take a stand every time we make a decision.

It would be burdensome and simply unnecessary to take stands whenever we act or speak. However, the knowledge that we gain about ourselves as we take stands helps us with the myriad little decisions we make daily. If we take a stand regarding food—say, not to eat more than one sweet per day—our choices in the grocery store or restaurant are informed by that overarching stand. Each Little League game missed by the family is not a big decision once the stand toward family vacations is made. Each time the classroom becomes momentarily noisy, the teacher responds without intense inner turmoil because he has taken his inner stand for quietness in his demeanor.

Many stands are of an everyday nature. Consider a sixty-year-old woman whom I will call Leah. Her doctor prescribed some medication for her to help her digestive system. The doctor explained that she was to take the medication one hour before breakfast. But daily she was awakened when her husband came to get her to eat the breakfast he had already prepared for her. He would give her the pill, then prod her to come and eat, for the toast was warm, the coffee made. She would sit at the table and begin to eat, then she would feel sick and would conclude that she simply was unable to eat in the morning. There would be some tension between them as both of them wished that she could eat better and both wondered what to do with the prepared breakfast. When lunchtime came, she was able to eat well, and things would be on a more even keel for the rest of the day.

Leah's middle-aged children were baffled. They asked why she didn't tell their dad that she couldn't eat for one hour after she took the pill. It didn't make sense to them that she would take the pill, eat, become ill, endure tension, and get upset every day. After hearing their arguments, she blurted out that life always includes some sacrifices. She could not ask him to change; the cost would be too great. She spoke up not to her husband but to her children. She took a stand as her values were being challenged: I will take the pill and immediately eat the prepared breakfast, regardless of the consequences. She valued health and honesty; but when she was forced to take a stand, her value for the avoidance of conflict with her husband in that particular situation became primary.

Leah's predicament is like that of many people in their various relationships. Leah's stand taking began when she challenged her own values, with conscious or perhaps unconscious reflection. She felt various internal pressures: I value my health; I value my husband; I value receiving love; I value not making waves; I value our relationship as it is. There were probably competing claims and emotions, such as the enjoyment of eating a lovingly prepared breakfast, anger at her husband for not understanding, a feeling of not being heard, and some ambivalence about how to meet her own health needs. Whether or not she gave much intentional thought to it, she arrived at the stand she took: I want things the way they are more than I want to speak up for change.

Leah's stand taking was forced into her conscious awareness when her adult children noticed her passive

stance. Then she had to sort through her values and
make public (to her children) her stand. Her stand was
a "sacrificial" one in that it was detrimental to her own
health. She feared the results of making a clear request
to her husband; she did not want to hurt him but was
willing thereby to hurt herself. Many people like her
need to learn how to speak up if they are going to live
as healthfully as possible and in genuinely reciprocal
intimate relationships. But in order to speak up, they
need to be willing to befriend conflict, to find out clearly
where they stand, and to accept the legitimacy of their
own power.

At the opposite end of the life cycle is Lyle, a twenty-
two-year-old man who has been dating for several
years. He has a first date with Clare coming up soon.
Since his breakup with his last girlfriend, over four
months ago, he has fine-tuned his own stand on appropriate sexual behavior. He has decided that he needs to
love and know the woman genuinely and to be able to
trust her commitment to him before he wants to have
sexual intercourse. In addition, he has become adamant
that the woman use contraception for herself and that
he use a condom. He has labored long and hard to
arrive at this inner stand, wrestling with his views of
love, health, and wholeness; his understanding of faith-
fulness to God and to others in relationships; and his
desire to be patient with his singleness, not to rush into
marriage prematurely.

If he and Clare do continue to date and grow to
experience love as they learn about each other, and if
Clare responds to Lyle without any challenge to his
stand, he may continue with his personal stand without
further reevaluation. But if Clare speaks up with a different position, Lyle will be forced to reassess his values
once again.

She, meanwhile, has her stands (labored over or lazily accepted), and if she does not speak up but acts against her own stands in favor of his, she has actually changed her stand. She has decided that the relationship or his lead is a more important value than her own stands had been. Speaking up affects each other's stands; speaking up involves risks, but it also offers the potential for genuine intimacy and integrity.

A woman who is deciding whether to speak up against her husband's alcoholism, to communicate that she will no longer support his addiction, will spend many hours agonizing over this stand she wants to initiate. It is wise for her to get the support of one who is experienced with alcoholic treatment programs as well as the support of people such as the family's clergy and colleagues at work. She will, if she holds to her stand, need to continue speaking up, in words and actions, until there is healing for her husband and their whole family.

All stands are interpersonal; every stand we take affects others in some way. Some things about which we want to speak up seem personal, such as a desire to attend school as an adult, while others involve huge systems, such as voting in a presidential election. Yet both the seemingly personal stands and those clearly involving systems do affect relationships. If you choose to go to school as an adult, you must negotiate how to arrange that with your family and friends. Your vote, and that of many others, affects many relationships owing to the policies of the person elected.

Practice in the smaller domains prepares us for speaking up in larger groups and systems. If a father has learned over time that it is permissible to say directly that he has a different opinion from his wife or children (and he is not put down or ignored), he is likely to be more confident in speaking up at a church committee meeting when he disagrees with a motion that has just been made. His confidence that his ideas matter transfers from one domain to the other.

Some of us are more forthright in larger domains—at the office, in the community, at church—but we turn into chameleons at home. We can easily say to colleagues that we disagree with their opinions; we can make our ideas known clearly and openly. But the stakes seem higher in intimate relationships, so we hem and haw when we state our opinions at home or we passively agree to whatever another says. Our speech is full of conviction at a pulpit or podium, but our words choke back tears when we talk with our best friend or spouse. We need to bring that trust and sincerity home.

In whatever domain we start our practice of speaking up, all other domains will be affected, for speaking up is empowering and creates an increased trust and tolerance of risk in all relationships.

Because there are unknowns involved, many people are reluctant to speak up. I appreciate the reluctance, for speaking up and taking stands have not come easily for me. Even today I experience ambivalence and wrestle to decide whether and how to speak. For me the journey toward attention to my stands and how I spoke them intensified during seminary. It became important for me to know what I believed and to be clear with others about my feelings and thoughts.

As the pastor of a church for four years I found myself needing to take stands that were new for me and in which conflict could not be avoided. I had either to speak up for inclusive language as we sang hymns or to remain silent. I spoke up and not everyone was happy, but we grew to understand one another as each of us reevaluated our stands. I had to speak up when a couple told me the day before their wedding that they would serve champagne at their wedding reception: The church's policy was not to; the couple said they had to.

After weighing my own values, I told the couple that they could not serve the champagne, for the stand of that church for years had been not to allow alcohol on the premises, and I needed to uphold that policy. I could not avoid speaking up unless I shirked my responsibility; I could not make everyone happy.

At the church I also had to decide whether to mention political concerns in my preaching. I chose to do so, using prudence and much searching for clarity on each position before I spoke. When some church members disagreed with me, the preaching evoked further discussion between us. We grew through our honest, passionate (and compassionate) ministry with one another. I was aware that my relationship with each church member and the members' relationships with other members were greatly affected by our collective speaking—our giving and receiving breath.

Speaking up is not a goal in itself. That is, we do not step out to find a stand but rather live in relationships, observing the necessity for stands in the midst of our interacting. Taking a stand does not guarantee correctness. It matters what the stand is—stands can be taken that are just plain wrong. For example, to stand for the oppression of another in a relationship is wrong, no matter how one speaks that stand.

Zeal is not the test of whether a stand is well said. With zeal parents could tell their college-aged daughter that she ought to become an engineer. It may be helpful to share that desire with the daughter, but to do so zealously does not make that speaking wiser. In fact, too much zeal may hurt the relationship or confuse the hearing.

At times we need to listen or to be silent. When we are with another person in a crisis, what is often needed is presence, not conversation or verbal consolation. Silence is far more golden than compulsive chatter overlying insecure feelings that emptiness would exist if words did not. Silence may be used as a discipline when one discovers that one talks very much about oneself. Silence is a marvelous discipline for professional talkers (preachers, teachers, politicians, and parents), in order to hear what those to whom we talk have to say. Silence is often valuable in the midst of an argument, when tempers are too hot and clarity is gone. Silence is useful when words have been said and said and said, but there is not yet a solution to a problem. The question is not listening or stand taking; we need both. Oftentimes we chatter to avoid both taking stands and enduring silence.

Once we launch into thinking about what it means to speak up, we realize that we have much to learn about ourselves. But we arrive at a point when we must also move outside ourselves, to imagine creatively what those to whom we speak think and feel. If we are going to be effective at speaking up, we need empathy to imagine walking in our hearer's shoes.

This book is intended to help you to speak up. If you speak up, you have a better chance of getting what you value. But speaking up brings no guarantees. Other people are involved in the process, so their values and desires are present too. You may not get exactly what you want, but the more you use your voice wisely, the more you *are* likely to discover genuine intimacy in your relationships. You will be more honest and will have more integrity, for you stand for what you are and believe in. When you speak up, you risk being misunderstood, but you will also grow in self-esteem. You may discover that you can effect change to help others, surprise yourself with a newfound sense of internal authority, and find the satisfaction that accompanies decisiveness. Holding your breath is neither needed nor wise. Sharing your voice generously and listening generously create an atmosphere of movement, freedom, spontaneity, and trust. Just as the peaceful swimmer enjoys the water, so we can enjoy giving and receiving breath.

For Reflection and Action

1. Consider several settings in your life right now in which you would like to speak up. When and how is it easy to speak? What makes it difficult?

2. Look for the stands you hold that you want to communicate in those situations. Notice what values those stands are based on.

3. Think about your own journey of stand taking. How have you progressed in speaking up in various domains, or what zigzag pattern of progress have you followed?

2

When You Are Afraid of Conflict

When we want to state our ideas and feelings to our loved ones, we are sometimes worried that they will become angry, so we hesitate to take the risk. Because we fear what could happen, we may avoid speaking at all. We think that an argument would create distance in the relationship. However, if we try to avoid conflict by not talking, that very avoidance creates distance. Instead of gaining intimacy, we create distance and lose intimacy by not speaking up.

Speaking up requires courage and is caring. It takes courage to speak out in an open way. I noted with fascination that a word translated as "courage" in the New Testament was, in the original Greek, *parrhesia,* a word that literally means "speaking out," or saying everything that needs to be said.[1] When we care deeply about an issue in a particular relationship or certain values in a large domain (such as keeping the environment free from toxic wastes), to speak up does require courage. If we do say everything that needs to be said, we can indeed be called courageous.

My son, who is four, recently became engaged with the Superman cartoons on Saturday mornings. As he sat screaming and coaching Superman from his seat on the sofa, he, like many viewers of suspenseful action, wanted to know how things would turn out. Finally it dawned on him that by the end of each show Superman is always safe. My son will now repeat several times during one half-hour show, "Mommy, Superman always ends up okay."

We would do well to maintain a willingness to risk adventurously in our relationships, with the expectation that we, too, will end up okay. Because we are not superhuman, of course we do not have guaranteed outcomes—we must face the unknown. But the spirit of facing odds and conquering them joyfully is worthy of maintaining well beyond age four.

Saying everything that needs to be said is not only courageous but also wise and caring. We may fear that we are being troublesome when we speak up, but we must convince ourselves that it is caring to do so. Naming issues that must be worked on can help a relationship grow.

The word "sin" is frequently identified with the definition I saw in a Sunday school crossword puzzle: "Doing something wrong." We think of sin as an act of commission—doing something we should not. But sin is estrangement from God, and we experience distance from our Source of Being by acts of omission—by not speaking or not taking action—just as surely as we do by inappropriate words and wrong acts.

Let us look at the stories of some people in the Bible who were courageous when they spoke out. They, like us, had no guarantee of the outcome. They risked the unknown even as they had some fear of it, but their care for their loved ones prompted them to speak.

Esther, whom we meet in the Hebrew Bible, had made it in many senses of the word. Although she was a Jew, she had not only entered into the king's court but had even been crowned as queen. She could have chosen to maintain the safety of her own position. When she found out that all the Jews in the kingdom were to be slain in eleven months, her first reaction was that she could do nothing. It would be too dangerous for her to go to the king unless he had specifically sent for her. But with the encouragement of her cousin Mordecai, she risked her own personal safety. She planned a set of dinners during which she asked the king to rescind the edict to kill the Jews, and he agreed. She *took a stand* to help her people.

Esther did not just accept her status, a hidden Jew who had made it in a racist society; she violated the status quo. She created a situation in which conflict could not be avoided. Did Esther create the conflict, or did she expose it?

Vashti was the queen before Esther, the one who did not obey the king. She would not come in to parade her beauty in front of the princes. She would not tolerate the humiliation of being scrutinized as a thing instead of a human being. She said no. She ruined the peace and was deposed. She *took a stand:* she created a situation in which conflict could not be avoided. Did Vashti create the conflict, or did she expose it?

Mordecai was the family member with ethical imperatives, the cousin and adviser of Esther who said, "Think not that in the king's palace you will escape any more than all the other Jews. For if you keep silence at such a time as this, relief and deliverance will rise for the Jews from another quarter, but you and your father's house will perish. And who knows whether you have not come to the kingdom for such a time as this?" (Esther 4:13–14). Did Mordecai create conflict for Esther by insisting that she act, or did he expose the fact that she was in the middle of it?

Speaking up when lives are at stake is an obvious act of courage. But more commonly, we have to gather courage to speak up in the midst of everyday conflicts. Thanksgiving Day, for instance, should be a time of family gratitude. But Richard remembered past Thanksgivings when tension mounted higher than the mashed potatoes. He recalled the anxieties and concerns of his wife, his mother, and his in-laws as they tried to get along, tried to bury years of disagreement. One year Richard suggested to his wife and mother that they try a different pattern for their celebration. Why not meet in two different gatherings, instead of one? Their family could get together on the eve of Thanksgiving, while the in-laws could come on Thanksgiving Day. Or the in-laws could come for a very special brunch, and their half of the family could gather for the evening meal. He knew that his speaking up was likely to create a situation in which the conflict would have to be acknowledged and faced. Did Richard create the conflict, or did he expose it?

Exposing conflict can bring forth healing and justice. Psychologist Jean Baker Miller has pointed out that most of the time the people who speak up are told that they create the conflict, but they rarely do. They expose the conflict that already exists but that those involved do not want to face.[2] Leah—whom we met in the first chapter—feared that she might create conflict between her husband and herself if she spoke up about their breakfast dilemma, but the conflict was there already. Her speaking would not have created conflict but would have exposed it.

The truth is that many attempts to "keep" peace do not bring peace. The attempts become ways to avoid intimacy, which of necessity includes conflict. To achieve genuine peace, one must "make" peace, and the path from false peacekeeping to genuine peacemaking is through the risk of conflict initiated by taking stands.

Those who believe that they gain from the avoidance of conflict are generally those who are oppressing others. This is a strong statement, but we can find many examples to sustain that observation. When black Americans were demonstrating for civil rights in the sixties, they were accused of creating conflict. Of course their accusers were also their oppressors, who were content with the status quo. Many Canadians are concerned about acid rain, which originates in electric power plants in the United States. Some Americans think that the Canadians, who are most affected by the oppressive conditions, are creating a conflict between peaceful neighbors. Those of us who are responsible do not want to name the conflict, for we might have to make changes in our way of doing things.

Oppression is a strong name for what occurs in interpersonal relationships; there can be debate about when it is occurring. Yet we see that, even between spouses who love each other, there can be an unjust distribution of a good and reluctance to discuss the issue on the part of the one who benefits from the status quo. For example, George is satisfied with the sexual expression in his marriage, but his wife, Lauren, is frustrated. She is hurt and feels discounted because George gets what he wants, but she is left feeling unimportant and used. George does not want to talk about their sexual interaction because he says they will only get upset at each other. But Lauren is already upset; for her, discussing their sexual expression holds out the only hope she has for improving it.

A hospital administrator may say that it is not a problem for employees to walk a third of a mile from their parking lot to the hospital entrance, while the employees insist that it is a problem. If a concern is declared "not a problem," those who are hurting are declared to be the ones creating the problem and are easily made to feel guilty for raising the issue.

In a family one member may declare to the others

that an issue is "not a problem," successfully stifling the whole family from finding a solution. In order to open the door for a solution, the family members of an alcoholic mother who denies her addiction must say to her, "Alcohol may not seem to be a problem for you, but it *is* a problem for us." Likewise, a wife must say to the husband who declares that they do not have any money problems, "Money may not be an issue for you, but it is a problem for me."

A general rule should be that if there is a problem for anyone in a relationship, it is a problem for the whole system. All are affected when one member is hurting. The hurting person has a right to speak up to make that hurt known.

We must accept the fact that life, the life God creates and declares to be good, necessarily includes conflict. Conflict is neutral: It cannot be judged good or bad of itself; it is simply a part of life. We may not experience conflict happily, but it is virtually always needed if there is to be growth or creativity in our own life or our relationships. If we avoid conflict when it does exist, we lose some degree of vitality, intimacy, and freedom.

Once we befriend conflict, we are able to risk having both closeness and independent action. When parents, for example, accept the fact that there is conflict in deciding how to raise children as a team, they can gain closeness in their relationship with each other in the midst of the conflict. As long as there is an overall coherence of values, they can be clear about their differences, recognizing that they are individuals and will do some things differently with their children. They are each more free and independent after they realize where they agree and disagree as a team.

Often, when we want to avoid conflict, we are clinging to a routine. Treasuring a routine simply for its own sake when that routine is not at all satisfying seems hollow, yet this value is really inherent in the avoidance of conflict much of the time. When we avoid conflict, we may do so thinking that we are valuing quiet, "niceness," or "politeness." But the ways in which we go about avoiding conflict are seldom nice and rarely honest.

Guidelines for Facing Conflict

When you find yourself on the verge of choosing *not* to speak because you are afraid of the possibility of having to face conflict, you may find it helpful to recall these five guidelines.

Seek realistic expectations. How do we take the leap to mention something that needs attention? We can gather more courage to speak if we are clear about realistic expectations. If I expect that whenever I take a stand I should get what I want, I will often be disappointed. Very seldom is it quite so simple. Desires have to be meshed with others' needs and wants; there has to be time for our stand to be heard and digested by the hearer. If we expect, as we speak up, that we are opening a topic or initiating a continuing dialogue on an issue, we can have the satisfaction that we have gotten our words out and have begun the process of hearing. We can then both persist with the topic and have times of patient silence—over a period of a few hours or even a number of months. The fact that we have to wait for a response or solution to the situation does not mean that we should not have spoken!

Seven years ago I spoke out at an institution that is important to me, telling the appropriate people that I thought we must do something to make the buildings accessible to those with handicapping conditions. At first I was admonished for raising the issue. Then a few

months later a task force was created to look into what
action could be taken, but the task force met rarely and
produced only minor changes in the buildings. Every
now and then I would raise the issue, asking what was
happening. Recently I saw some concrete action being
taken. I was grateful, though the effort is far from
completed.

During those years I felt a mixture of feelings: embar-
rassment for having put into words what some leaders
did not want mentioned, anger at those who were not
paying attention to the concern, persistence (I had
made my stand; I was going to hold to my position),
impatience, impotence, and sadness for the people having trouble moving about the buildings. There were
others who spoke out during those years too; our voices
together impacted the system's change of attitude.

The scenario can be similar for intimate relationships. We cannot expect someone to hear our novel idea
with complete openness if it is a request for a change
on that person's part. But this does not mean we should
not speak. We can find ways to make our values and
wants known as clearly and as calmly as possible, and
then be patient while persisting.

As we try to have realistic expectations in our speaking, it is helpful to think of the process that is occurring
as a desire moving toward fulfillment. We would like
events to move from *desire* to *fulfillment* to *calm.* But
often events move from *desire* through *conflict* and
struggle before they reach *fulfillment* and *calm.* When
we speak up, we may find fulfillment soon thereafter,
with no conflict. But far more frequently there are conflict and struggle—these are just part of the natural
process.

Family therapist Walter Kempler recalled a couple
who desired to have a calm evening in spite of the fact
that there was an issue over which they had a present

conflict. They did not want to spoil a pleasant evening with a quarrel. But, he suggests, if their quarrel is avoided (as the couple pretends there is no conflict), completion is not really achieved.[3] There are desire and a pretense of calm—no real fulfillment and no real calm.

This couple could face the conflict and agree to have a brief quarrel, to get out into the open what they need to say. Then they might be able to move to the other side of their conflict and reach a genuine calm, not the tense quiet of avoidance. They do not have to reach the final conclusion of their debate, but they can get off their chests what they must in order to be fully present to each other. Pretending that nothing is wrong makes it difficult for them to be together.

When my mother's income was altered and she wanted to readjust her Social Security benefits, she desired a simple, straightforward process. But there were struggle, conflict, and questioning before the agencies and the personal tallies agreed and all were satisfied. If she had quit her pursuit of a correct solution in order to avoid conflict, she would probably have sacrificed some of her benefits. She has never liked conflict, but her willingness to pursue her goal despite inevitable conflict helped her not only financially but also emotionally. She was not left resentful and upset about an inadequate and unjust solution.

When we start with a desire and accept the struggle and conflict that arise, we may arrive at fulfillment: the correct Social Security adjustment, the institutional commitment to accessibility, the couple's conclusion to their argument. Yet it is possible that, rather than fulfillment and calm, there are grief and calm. The couple might have to grieve over the loss of a hoped-for solution if they cannot easily find fulfillment from their struggle. If these people had not faced their struggles, they could not be calm; they would keep mumbling inwardly about their concerns. Once they have struggled—with loved ones or with agencies—there can be calm, even if grief becomes a necessary part of the process.

Observe your motives for speaking. A second guideline for speaking when you are afraid of conflict is to observe yourself and your motives for speaking. Ungluing ourselves from our own way of seeing things is a virtue that is strongly advocated within the Judeo-Christian tradition; we are encouraged to move beyond ourselves to see as others (or God) might see. This caution to stop, to try to see our views or actions from another perspective than our own, is a good check on whether or not to speak up—and how to do this. Certainly Esther's first thoughts were for her own safety: It is not safe to go to the king with this request. But with the encouragement of her friends and family, she was helped to see beyond her own needs to a much wider picture. Not only was she asked to sacrifice her own safety or needs, she was also challenged to reevaluate her values, and her genuine stand became one of speaking up.

When you hear yourself say something like, "I don't want to mention this to my father, even though it's for his own good, because he might get angry," or, "I never speak up in the meeting, because they may not like my ideas," you may be trying to keep a false peace. What may be needed is peace at a deeper level, which can be achieved only with some effort. You may be surprised to find that others are willing to take some effort too.

When I am most convinced that I am right, I have the least tendency to try to move beyond my view of things. I am so sure I am right that I do not even realize my view could be challenged. So it is not only when we have doubt or uncertainty that we need to look at ourselves, but especially when we are convinced of our position. The king, for example, was probably quite convinced that he was right in asking Vashti to parade herself; he probably had not tried to see the situation from her perspective.

While I have assumed that most people do not speak up because they are afraid of conflict and have not really accepted the fact that conflict is a necessary—and potentially wholesome—aspect of life, I realize that some people are apparently *not* afraid of conflict. Some seem even to enjoy conflict and to create it frequently, whether or not there is any potentially healthy outcome. The pause to look beyond ourselves is a guide that helps us either to quell our too-frequent speaking or to have courage to say what needs to be said.

Make "I Statements." A frequently suggested guideline for communicating is to make "I statements." When a father thinks it is appropriate to alter the time by which his teenager must be home, he makes an I statement to his wife by saying something like, "I have been thinking—it seems to me that we could lengthen Bob's curfew time by an hour." His wife can hear the message clearly: The husband thinks there should be a change. There is no judgment toward the wife and no reason for her to be upset by the message itself. He is not blaming anyone for the way things have been; he is simply saying that he thinks there should now be adjustments.

This way of speaking is much more constructive than vague or accusatory statements such as: "You know, you and I were out later than Bob is when we were his age," or "Why don't you let Bob stay out later now that he is older?" By making these comments, the husband does not clearly state *his* stand; his values are not exposed. In the first instance, the wife is left to guess what the husband means when he comments about what they did at Bob's age. In the second, the husband is passing the need for a stand on to his wife, though the fact that he is bringing up the subject clearly suggests that he has a stand on the issue.

I have observed that many stands people take are statements of passions or clear wants. I want buildings to be accessible. The husband wants the family to update the rules as the children grow. My mother wanted to get her finances settled. Richard wanted an enjoyable Thanksgiving with his loved ones. None of these people spoke up out of anger. They wanted a change but were not initially angry about what had been; they just perceived that something should now be different.

Yet the receiver of a communicated stand often immediately assumes that the speaker is angry. "You don't think I'm flexible enough?" the wife may say, as she thinks her husband is angry about the rule. "You don't like our family gatherings?" Richard's family might respond when he suggests the change in plans. "Are you trying to damage our image?" respond the leaders of the institution that was not accessible. None of these three responses is called for if the message is heard as a want, a positive passion on the part of the speaker.

Yet there is nothing that the speaker can do to ensure that the hearer will hear only the want or the passion. Because the hearer has personal vulnerabilities, she or he may hear anger where there is none, no matter how clearly the speaker talks. However, when speakers are extremely clear that the desires are theirs and that they want to hear the hearers' opinions too, there is more likelihood that the message will be heard simply as a request, not as an attack on the hearers.

It is helpful if speaker and hearer do not automatically jump to the conclusion that one must win while the other loses. Even the king and Vashti might have been able to work out a compromise if the king did not *have* to win. When statements are made that start out, "You need to change this . . . ," the hearer can easily feel that she or he is in a competitive exercise. But if the statement begins, "I have thought about this, and I think . . . ," there is more probability that the hearer can attend to the wants, the desires of the speaker, not the imminent fear of loss. In almost every situation in which a stand is taken, it is possible for all parties to benefit, to feel cared for, to grow. But it may take much talking and hearing to arrive at that awareness and at a solution.

Consider seriously mentioning the "unmentionable." An observation that has helped me speak when I was afraid to do so is that what is not said is experienced somehow anyway, though usually in a confused fashion. When there is a problem in a relationship, conflict is present whether or not it is mentioned. Talking about it is very likely a relief from the burden of not naming it and keeping quiet about what is known.

Esteemed counselor Carl Rogers, in his book *Becoming Partners,* recollected in describing his own forty-seven-year marriage, "We seem to have realized that the thing which cannot *possibly* be revealed to the other *can* be revealed, the problem which *you must keep* to yourself can be shared."[4]

An example of this phenomenon is the Rose family, whose child-care arrangements with former spouses are getting in the way of their current marriage. The Roses know this fact, but they have not dared to talk about their concerns, because their past marriages are taboo subjects for them. Each knows that the problem exists;

their not mentioning it does not eliminate or solve it. Since the situation is present, even if it is not mentioned, they might try sharing their concerns and desires about what they think cannot possibly be revealed.

In group settings conflict can be present even when it is not mentioned, just as it is in intimate one-to-one relationships. In a counseling group of mostly single people, the leader managed to turn the discussion to some other topic whenever any member mentioned marriage. At first the group members were not conscious of what was happening, but eventually there developed a sense that the group was avoiding the topic of marriage. Yet no one named the avoidance. One day the leader confessed to them that he was having great problems in his own marriage. All of a sudden it was clear what had been happening: The leader was so upset about his own marriage that he had deliberately avoided letting the group talk about marriage in general.

The members felt the avoidance. Once they could talk with the leader openly, they could allay many of the leader's fears about how they perceived him, and they could challenge him, too. Although the group thought they could not possibly mention their perception that the leader was intentionally avoiding discussion about marriage, the leader needed to tell them what he was going through; they might have been able to help him. The effect on the group when the leader finally spoke was much better than his (and their) avoidance of the issue.

Churches can have two or more subgroups within their membership. The people know this fact but resist naming the division for fear of splitting the church. Yet the surest way to split a church (or any group) is not to mention that the subgroups exist until it is too late.

Naming what all clearly see anyway has a therapeutic effect on the membership. Once they are allowed to name the problem, they can find some solutions.

Sometimes a community avoids naming a difficulty the community itself poses for a person with a handicapping condition. For example, there may be a member of the community who is deaf. For a variety of reasons, the members avoid naming the problem that person is obviously having as a participant in the community. People are not sure how this person feels, since he communicates very little. Some members fear that they should not draw too much attention to the one who cannot hear. Others just do not take the time to consider his needs. Not naming the problem and the need for additional resources within the community does not make the problem go away. It simply hurts even more the one who is suffering the most from the avoidance of conflict. If members named the needs (such as interpreters, understanding how to telephone deaf persons, learning sign language, inviting other deaf members), feelings, issues, and perhaps conflict would emerge, but the one member would not have to suffer because of the others' avoidance.

I would not arbitrarily advise everyone to risk sharing with another. I do not think we must know everything, even about our spouses. The boss does not need to know all the workers' feelings, nor do the workers need to hear all the employer's views. It is important to check out the motivation behind the desire to communicate.

Issues that clearly affect the current relationship are present and are shared in nonverbal ways. Talking will definitely require courage and will interrupt the routine, but giving the situation words is a step in the right direction.

Trust the potential for grace in a relationship. A married couple in a counseling situation discussed with me the way they tended to avoid arguing even when they knew that they were at odds with each other. I asked them what their experiences had been at the end of their previous arguments. Were the endings of previous arguments filled with grace, understanding, and acceptance of each other, or were the endings only distancing, with little obvious good to be found? They recollected instances of each type but realized that the more painful memories had clouded over the memories of their forgiving and reconciling endings of arguments.

Clearly, our past track record with conflict in a relationship encourages or discourages us from taking the risk of facing it once again.

I was raised to avoid conflict. My twin sister and I were isolated from each other when we were found to be arguing, and that was a large punishment for us. I can understand this strong reinforcement of the avoidance of conflict on my mother's part because she was still remembering her father's shouting at her mother during her own childhood. My mother's past experience of too much shouting led her not to want anything like that in her home again. My experience at not being allowed to argue at all led me to be afraid of it but also to want the freedom to engage in it!

When my husband and I first moved to Dayton, we had been married for almost three years. An incident occurred that resulted in a flurry of raised voices. He told me that something I had just done had not shown consideration of him. I responded that I had not realized what he had needed or what I had done. We were both very honest, hurt, puzzled, yet caring. Ten minutes later we were friends; I was amazed. That experience led me to understand the concept of grace in a more complete way. Neither of us was right or wrong.

We both took stands to express our genuine feelings to the other. At the moment of conflict, our values for honesty and sharing feelings were very high, while our values for routine and politeness were not.

The potential for grace is what enables us to speak up. The married couple who were counseling with me needed to feel deeply the grace in their relationship. They had had moments of it. They could remember times when they had faced an issue and disagreed but had continued speaking until they knew once again that they loved each other. Recalling those times, they now trust grace more and fear conflict less.

We can hold on to images of grace events in the past when we are about to speak up again. I still shake, turn cold, and get numb hands when I am about to risk conflict, especially in a faculty meeting or a public forum, but I do it when I am convinced that I must take a stand, precisely because I trust that grace.

Many times I do not need to remind myself about that grace in order to speak, but when I am particularly afraid to speak, I use my imagination to remember graceful outcomes of other times when I spoke. The more we speak up, the more of these graceful events we can collect in our memories to use for further encouragement in speaking.

For Reflection and Action

1. Think about the way you face and avoid conflict. Consider several situations in which conflict existed, whether or not it was named; notice your actions in those settings. Now consider two alternative choices you could have made, exploring the possible outcomes of the alternatives in your mind.

2. Observe yourself for a day to note how you communicate to others, especially whether you make "I

statements" such as, "I would like this," or "I think you look smashing today." If you do not include the "I," how do you say what you mean, and what possible effect does that have on the hearers?

3. Recollect graceful outcomes to several conflict situations in which the conflict was faced and discussed.

3

When You Are Not Sure Where You Stand

Scenario Number One: I am speechless, thinks a father as his teenagers ask him for permission to go to an all-night party. Scenario Number Two: Donna's husband comes home and says, "I was asked to move again, to take a job promotion in Cincinnati. What do you think?" Scenario Number Three: A man who considers himself a responsible citizen is getting ready to vote in tomorrow's election. He must decide whether he is willing to increase taxes to help provide housing for the homeless.

Many times we are not sure where we stand. We sincerely want to speak up, and we have to give an answer, but we do not know what to say. We may give as much conscious attention to our values as we can in the short space of time we have to speak up. Or we may give an answer without really looking squarely at our reasons—our stand becomes a knee-jerk reaction rather than a well-thought-through coalescing of values.

Some obvious factors influence the stands we take both in our relationships and in the public sphere. Whether we are female or male, how healthy we are physically, and what color we are affect our ways of seeing. We are influenced by the views of our families of origin, whether we agree with our parents' values or not. Unique personal experiences alter our values. For instance, if we have at some time in our lives spent a year looking for employment and living on food stamps, our views about others in that situation will be affected. Whereas, if we have never looked for a job but, rather, had them seemingly come to us, we may perceive that jobs are abundant and available for all. If we have been pregnant when we did not want to be, how we and our families responded to that crisis will affect our stands for others in that situation. Our view of sex education and birth control will be influenced by that experience of pregnancy. Looking at the world with less or more money affects how we see others and ourselves—we panic about different things, and our faith is tested differently.

The books, newspapers, and magazines we read influence our values and offer suggested stands. Some people are illiterate; written resources are not accessible to them. Those who are bilingual are able to grasp the values inherent in language itself as they are influenced by two modes of thought. If we have traveled abroad, what we have seen will enable us to expand our grasp of viable stands to take. Any travel—even to different parts of the United States—expands our ideas and stretches our values.

Our life stage will influence our values and our speaking, for we see things differently according to how we view the past and the future. We recall how "we used to do things," and we have hopes for the future. Life-altering events such as marriage, having children, changing careers, and becoming divorced or widowed can impact our values and transform our stands.

Our religious upbringing is a large source of guidance in establishing stands from which to speak. Even if we did not attend church or synagogue regularly, we have been influenced by the religion of our families, our neighborhood, and our larger community.

We may use these accumulated resources and give

intense thought to making some of our stands, yet much of what we say has not been considered with a good deal of intentional thought. We can even develop stands in an unconscious manner; we are not sure how we came to our views or why. We give an answer to the teenager, the spouse, or the ballot and realize later that we don't really hold the stands we thought we held. For example, we thought we stood for basic housing and health care for every person, but we were not quite willing to pay for that. Or we thought we stood for mobility and change for professional success, but we begin to realize that other values are equally important.

A good deal of counseling with families or couples includes enabling people to make their stands conscious, to evaluate their stands, and to communicate those stands clearly to one another. In the midst of the discovery or the communication, the stands may indeed be changed, for as each person stops holding his or her breath and starts giving it to the other, all can receive, give, and receive again and again, and each is transformed in the interchange.

Psychotherapists from a variety of schools of thought agree that it is healthy for individuals and relationships for us to make our unconscious stands conscious. For one thing, we can be far more "congruent" with one another. Congruence in geometry occurs when two figures match each other exactly; they are the same shape and size. Congruence for humans occurs when our actions match our values.

I am not congruent when I think that I hold one stand consciously, but I actually practice another stand. For example, if I think that I stand for accessibility, but I enter building after building having no qualm as I see people struggle with canes and crutches to reach the top of the steps and do nothing to communicate my stand, I really do not hold the stand I thought I did for accessibility. The stand from which I am acting is: "Only able-bodied people need to enter easily; others do not need to enter or can struggle to do so."

If we realize that we do not hold the stand we thought we did, since our actions prove differently, we may be chagrined. We begin to sort out: Do I have to change my view of myself or my actions? This is often painful, so we may pull forth what psychologists call "defense mechanisms," actions or ways of thinking that protect us from being fully aware of what we are doing. We create defense mechanisms when we think that we cannot face the truth and survive—physically or emotionally.

Defending Against Knowing Where We Stand

Three defenses in particular are important for us to recognize when we are trying to determine what it is we want to speak forth. They are "denial," "projection," and "introjection."

Denial. If I climbed the stairs and really did not see the struggle of those with crutches, I would have denied myself an understanding of the experience of the other climbers, but I would also have denied the existence of my own inner stand.

Someone could use denial as a defense mechanism against precaution in sexual expression. He or she may engage in sex with several partners over a short period of time but block off any thoughts that this behavior is potentially dangerous. He or she may have heard and read about sexually transmitted diseases and may have the knowledge that the best precaution against acquiring AIDS through sexual means is to have one partner at a time with whom one uses precautions such as condoms. But that knowledge is irrelevant if the person denies his or her own practices.

Much of the success in reducing the spread of AIDS in the gay community has come from education in that community to enable each person to be *conscious* about what stands he is taking in any relationship regarding sexual behavior—not to deny what he is doing or risking.

At the beginning of this chapter I mentioned Donna, who was approached by her husband with the question about what she thought of moving to Cincinnati if he were to accept a promotion in his work. Many values will affect her response: her love for and satisfaction with her own work, the impact of the move on their children, how much change is beneficial within a certain period of time for the family as a whole and each member individually, the pace and quality of life in both settings, the financial factors involved in the move and change of jobs, connections with church or religious communities, distance from extended family and friends.

Under the pressure of the request, Donna may deny some of these values even to herself. A particular event or value may not occur to her consciously. If it arises, she may discount it as not important in the consideration. For example, there may have been very stressful times with the children during the last two moves, but she may deny that as she recollects. Or she may value stability as much as change, but, because she feels pressure to change, she will deny that she treasures stability of place. She may even deny her love for and commitment to her own work.

Projection. When we show a film using a movie projector, it looks as if the picture is on the screen, when in fact the source of the picture is the film within the projector itself. Likewise, when we think some feeling or attitude is in another person, but it is actually inside ourselves rather than being in that person, we are projecting our experience onto him or her. If projection is occurring, we do not realize that the feeling is our own; we think it comes from the other.

Anger is often a feeling that is projected onto another rather than being recognized within oneself. "Mary is angry at me" could be what Susan really believes, when in fact Mary is not at all angry, but Susan is angry with Mary. Love can also be projected, so that Evan thinks that Penny loves him when she thinks of him only as a friend; instead, he is in love with her and not willing to admit it.

The speechless father of Scenario Number One, when asked by his teenagers for permission to go to an all-night party, may use projection to get out of accepting responsibility for thinking through the stand on his own. He may say, "Your mother would say it's all right." He puts the responsibility on the mother instead of acknowledging that he is giving permission.

One clue to projection is speech patterns that are passive in nature. Whenever I hear someone say, "I am getting married to so-and-so," I listen closely to see if projection is occurring. I do not worry if the person can just as accurately say, "I am marrying so-and-so." "I am marrying" is a conscious stand; but "I am getting married" is a passive statement, indicating that the future spouse is taking a stand, but the speaker may not be.

Clearly, people use words in idiomatic ways. When a person uses an occasional passive phrase, she or he may not be passive about the decision at all. The statement can be tested by making it active to see whether it is as accurate as the passive one.

The husband of a couple who have been married fifteen years is feeling distant from his wife now she has begun working full time while maintaining many volunteer involvements. He does not want her to be gone from him so much and is feeling uncared for and lonely. But he has never considered himself dependent on her and has told her many times that she has a right to work just as he does. He literally does not allow his feelings of abandonment and dependency to enter into his awareness, for this would be threatening to his view of himself. Yet the feelings are there. So what evolves is an unconscious stand: "You don't get my love when you work so much."

Because he is unaware of his feelings and his inner stand, he cannot tell his wife about them. She does not know that he is upset, but she does begin to realize that he is withdrawing his affection from her. When she asks what is wrong, he sincerely says, "I'm not feeling distant from you; you're the one who is feeling upset." He has projected the feelings of distance and upset onto her. He really believes that the distance is her fault, when the feelings are actually his. She was feeling closer to him, for she was active and eager to discuss her activities with him once she reunited with him after work, but he was unable to see this because his vision was clouded by his own unrecognized feelings.

Projection leaves people confused about who is feeling what. If the husband became aware of his feelings and his inner stand, he would have to take responsibility for his actions and for his need for her. His facing those natural feelings would be a movement toward a good solution for the couple, but it is threatening for him to acknowledge the feelings.

Introjection. When we use the third defense mechanism, introjection, we take on what is someone else's

stand, using it as if it were our own without examining
whether we really want it. The voter of Scenario Number Three uses introjection if he consults the editors of
his local newspaper to see how they say to vote and
decides to vote in agreement with the paper's editorial,
without checking out his own opinions in relation to
their arguments. If he mentally chewed on those arguments and thought about his own ideas and values, his
vote would be his own, even if he ended up agreeing
with the editorials.

I visualize what happens during introjection as a
snake that has just swallowed a rat. The rat is not
assimilated into the body of the snake; it is apparent to
the observer that a foreign body is inside the reptile. If
I just swallow what has been told me by my church, my
political affiliation, and my parents or teachers, I too
have not chewed to assimilate the stand. It is someone
else's stand sitting inside me, even though I think it is
my own.

It would make parenting, preaching, and teaching
much easier if children, congregants, and students
would just introject what the parents, preachers, and
teachers say. A parent says, "Do your homework," so
the little girl does her homework. A preacher says,
"Make sure you do something to serve your community," so the layperson decides to work at the food
bank. The teacher says, "Organize your paragraphs in
this manner," so the student writes as the teacher explains. If the child, layperson, and student are introject-
ing, they not only obey those in authority but really
believe they want to do their homework, serve the community, and organize their paragraphs in the prescribed
fashion.

Eventually the time may come when the introjected
material is genuinely digested and actually becomes a

part of the one who acts. The little girl may choose to do her homework because *she* stands for doing homework. The layperson distributes food out of a belief that the action makes for a better world. The student organizes the writing as suggested because that works well. But the student may let go of the introjected value at times in order to try a creative piece of poetry. Most parents, teachers, and preachers sincerely want those to whom they talk to chew on the stands, to fit them to their own experiences.

A disturbing example of introjection in an interpersonal relationship occurs between a girl and boy as stand taking over sexual behavior. Researchers have sought to find the rate of consistency between sexual values and sexual behavior. There seems to be more consistency for men. Men's sexual guilt and behavior match—are congruent—more often than those of women.[1] Women are more likely to have a consciously held stand against certain sexual behaviors but to do them anyway. Along with this research is the not-too-surprising discovery that "men have a great deal of influence on couples' contraceptive behavior."[2]

The women who have the highest guilt over being sexually active use the defense mechanism of denial to avoid admitting their sexual desires. Therefore, a woman like this is not prepared with contraception because she does not imagine herself as one who would be sexually active. But at the moment of necessity, she "introjects" her male partner's stand, allowing his attitude to become hers. "It's OK; we're in love." "Trust me, you won't get pregnant." "If you love me, you'll do this."

Women who have high sex guilt *and* insist on a stand for no sex or sex with contraceptives are congruent. Women who do not have high sex guilt, admit their sexual desires, and take responsibility for the desires are also congruent. The problem comes when women deny their desires, yet, in the moment of necessity, introject the man's stands. These women may have high sex guilt, yet they become pregnant without wanting to.[3]

To let go of their introjections, these women must be able to establish a sense of their own capacity to choose and to implement those choices. As they do this, they differentiate their own choices from those of the men. In this process both partners discover their own stands regarding their sexual behavior and courageously use their internal power to communicate that to the other. Neither acts out of the other's stands, betraying her or his own.

Recovering Our Hidden Stands

When we want to speak up responsibly, fully aware of what we are standing for, in addition to consulting all the various obvious sources of wisdom (religion, literature, family values), we can consult our unconscious. We can seek to make the unconscious conscious, gently moving away the defenses we have created that hide our real positions. There is a variety of ways in which we can tease forth the wisdom and truth from our friend the unconscious.

Notice surprise reactions to change. Sometimes a new awareness emerges because of a change in the routine in a relationship. For instance, we make many simple stands in relation to eating. He likes potatoes— four times a week at least, she thinks. She eats them because he wants them. Then he leaves for a four-month tour of duty, and she discovers herself craving potatoes. It dawns on her during this time that she has been wanting the potatoes all along. She had been projecting the desire onto him, unaware that she likes potatoes. She lets go of her projection when she acknowledges to herself her own desires.

Meanwhile, while he is away he discovers that he shuns those vegetables his wife has said he loves. He realizes that he does not like potatoes very much—never did; she seemed to like them, and he began to believe that it was his desire, not hers. He undoes his introjection when he faces his true likes and dislikes rather than taking on what she says he likes.

Try speaking actively. If we notice that we speak passively or noncommittally, we may be avoiding taking stands ourselves by putting them onto others instead. Each time we hear ourselves say such things as, "Do you want to go to a movie?" we can check whether we are really saying, "I want to go to a movie now," or "I really don't want to go anywhere tonight." We can hear ourselves say, "It certainly matters to my husband that our children attend Sunday school," and ask ourselves, "Do I, also, want them to attend but have not said so, since I let him speak on this matter?"

When we take back what we have projected onto others, we are really befriending and accepting rejected parts of ourselves. A homecoming of sorts is occurring. We get ourselves back with a wider range of feelings, attitudes, and experiences.

Ask friends for honest perceptions. We can ask friends how they perceive us, using them as mirrors to help us see ourselves. A friend may say, "I know you say you have dealt with your grief, but I think you seem to be still a bit disoriented and in shock." This friend is offering an observation that could help us face feelings of grief we have denied. Of course, anything friends say needs to be tested by checking our own thoughts and reflections. Sometimes, however, friends see much about us that we do not, yet without our request or permission they will not tell us.

Pay attention to nighttime dreams. Sometimes our dreams will picture us doing things or being in situations that are quite unlike what we think of ourselves. The nighttime dreams may be an inner mirror, tugging at us in playful and exaggerated ways to see some denied aspect.

I had a dream that had me enlisted in a battle scene in which I was shooting at people. When I reflected on the dream, I was a bit upset to have seen myself shooting with a gun, for I think of myself consciously as a peaceful person. But I realized that I do shoot people down at times in my mind, discounting some of their good qualities; also, I shoot people down verbally. This uncomfortable dream forced me to face and reflect on my tendency toward being judgmental.

Dreams do not just mirror problem areas for us that we had denied; they also reveal potentials that we are denying. A common dream theme is that of discovering an additional room on one's house. I recall a man who told of having such a dream and took it as a small form of guidance to trust his new creative adventure in his profession. I have also had dreams such as this; when I do I feel more confident that my future is to be increasingly creative—with more doors to open.

Intentionally seek guidance from God. Since God speaks to us through our bodies, we can listen to our body wisdom for messages we have been denying. (If our body has communicated stress for a long while, it is time to make some changes.) But God also speaks through our reasoning capacities, so we can attend to rational thought and reflection, seeking to be open to God in that way.

God's avenues of speech are manifold. God speaks through our imagination, and we can also enlist that resource for guidance. Prayer can include time for images to emerge spontaneously, as we ask for guidance about ourselves and our relations.

Often images are comical or dramatic, almost as if they were bold precisely in order to get our attention. For example, if a miser appears in our imagery prayer, we may ponder how we are miserly to others or ourselves *or* the opposite—how we are denying the need to hold on to our own things or values. We may give of ourselves too generously, without an adequate sense of our own worth.

If we see ourselves in the imagery with no clothes on, we may ask whether we are needing to disclose something to ourselves or others. Or we may realize that we fear facing something in a relationship, for we are afraid that it will leave us completely vulnerable, able to be seen with no coverings.

Another way to seek guidance is to sit in intentional silence. Sitting in silence can be one of the best ways to learn about ourselves. If I try to still my thoughts, what does cross my mind tends to be what preoccupies me. That flow of thoughts gives me clues to my true feelings and values.

At first many people tend to fear discovering what they may find in their unconscious. But the more we see of our depths, the more we are likely to befriend what is within. It becomes a good thing to discover what we stand for, now we are no longer afraid to look. If we find stands that are not in keeping with our self-images, we can take a serious look at ourselves nondefensively to see if we need to update our images or to make the stands more realistic.

The more we befriend what is within, the more we are likely to live courageously as full human beings with one another. We do not blame others for being a certain way, for we acknowledge a common humanity. We become kinder to all because we have faced the complexity within our very souls. As we become more complete, we have more creative energy and hope, for the resources within are mighty when they become available to us.

For Reflection and Action

1. Record some dreams you have at night and reflect to see whether they mirror you as you are in the daytime or whether they offer some other picture of yourself. Playfully toy with the image that is in the dream to see whether it offers any new ideas about yourself and your inner values or stands. If you are interested in pursuing personal work with dreams, consult a book such as Jeremy Taylor's *Dream Work.*

2. Ask two friends what they believe you stand for. Try to hear them nondefensively; then discuss with them how their perceptions match your view of yourself. If there are discrepancies, reflect on whether they are caused by incongruities between your thoughts and behaviors or by your friends' limited perceptions based on limited observance of you.

3. Choose a new way to pray, perhaps a style that uses imagery or more silence than you have usually tried. You may be interested in my book *Prayer on Wings: A Search for Authentic Prayer* (San Diego: Lura Media, 1990).

4

When You Don't Think
You Have Enough Power

The young girl who is able to tell her gymnastics teacher that she would prefer to work on the floor exercises instead of the bars because she has blisters on her hands believes she has the power to influence her world and the people in her world will hear her and respond.

The man who is able to say directly to his wife, "I surely would like to have a child soon. What do you think about that?" is also naming his wants clearly and acting as if he has legitimate power in a relationship in which his wife's desires will, of course, be important for the decision too.

In order to speak up in relationships, it is necessary to have a solid sense of our own power. We must recognize, accept, and use our power. Speaking is powerful. We are presenting ourselves to others and expecting them to make room in their lives for our ideas. I appreciate psychologist Jean Baker Miller's definition of power as "the capacity to implement."[1] When we speak up, we are accepting some responsibility for implementing action.

There may be times in our lives when we doubt we have the capacity to implement in a particular relationship, so we remain quiet when we really would like to speak. A man may want a child but not believe he has the power to affect that decision in his relationship with a woman. An elderly woman may want to stay in her own home but not feel powerful enough to say so clearly to the children and social workers who are beginning to make alternative housing arrangements for her.

We can empower ourselves and one another. Some people who have felt themselves to be voiceless for years are able to gain sufficient power to speak. A young mother who had stayed in a battering marriage for ten years reported, "You know, I used to only hear his words, and his words kept coming out of my mouth. He had me thinking that I didn't know anything. But now, you know, I realize I'm not so dumb. . . . And my own words are coming out of my mouth now."[2]

The experience of having a say, having a voice, is the experience of power. I can make a change; my opinion matters; I will be heard.

I recall my secret pleasure when I could calmly and nonapologetically tell neighborhood children who had been playing for a while at our house, "It's time to go home now." I was the mother, the one with systemic power in that intergenerational relationship of parents and children, but I had to gather courage to speak, to believe that no one would be offended by my implementing a necessary action. I have improved in my ability to speak to neighborhood children, just as I learned in earlier stages of my life to speak in school and work settings. We do not need to stay stuck in powerless or apologetic modes of expression.

In our culture women tend to have more trouble speaking up in public than men do, and African Americans and other ethnic minorities within a white system have more trouble speaking up. Therefore, if all of us are going to have a say and benefit from hearing every person's voice, women and people of color have to work harder to speak, and men and whites have to listen harder. Women of color, whose voices are least heard, need to speak and to be listened to most acutely.

Although statistically females have greater verbal ability than males from an early age, girls learn quickly to be reluctant to state their opinions fully; they are more tentative than boys.[3] Even when women hold strongly to their own views, they are often so concerned with not hurting the feelings of others that they do not express dissent. They report that they are "apt to hide their opinions and then suffer quietly the frustration of not standing up to others."[4]

Females in our culture are reinforced in their avoidance of their own power. Not openly expressing dissent is applauded as being cooperative, and not risking hurting others is seen as being self-sacrificial. Some men, too, may remain silent, fearing that if they speak they will hurt someone, but in general men are not as incapacitated in speaking for this reason. Neither do they have quite the same fear of ostracism for having spoken. For men, being seen as outspoken is not felt pejoratively, as it is for many women.

In the past few decades considerable attention has been given to how women in our culture experience power and how women can gain a clearer sense of their identities. Men realize now, too, that they can no longer assume the status quo in their various roles. Where many men used to enjoy strength projected onto their silences at home, they are now learning how to speak their own words. When it is no longer assumed that men do certain things while women do others, men and women have to find out what they *do* want and must talk in order to find mutually acceptable arrangements. Like the women who have had to wrestle with finding their voices in public spheres, men who do not accept past stereotypical roles discover that they need to find their wants and voices at home.

The capacity to implement is complex and requires much honesty and self-reflection. A clergywoman and her husband, who was not a clergyman, were sharing with a group of friends her recent appointment to a new church. The husband wanted to make several changes in the new parsonage to accommodate his hobbies. In particular, the husband wanted to build a workroom in the garage, but he did not know how to go about asking for permission. He felt awkward, since it was his wife's employers' home. He wondered what power he had to make his request heard.

He told his friends that wives of ministers had learned to get what they wanted indirectly, by using "manipulation." He felt he did not know how to manipulate the situation, but neither did he feel the power to ask directly. The group groaned at his comment that ministers' wives managed to get what they wanted through manipulative means. They empathized with his feelings of powerlessness, but they were upset, too, by the situation that the wives had been in.

This episode shows a variety of concerns. The husband envied what he perceived as the wives' capacity to work behind the scenes. Yet the wives surely had not enjoyed resorting to using those means, if in fact they had. Their frustrations were quite like this man's when they wanted to have their concerns heard, but they too may not have known how to go about speaking up in their situations. Some wives probably were able to get what they wanted, but no doubt many were unsuccessful.

The goal surely should not be for this man to learn manipulative means because he thinks he has no voice but, rather, for him to claim his voice, and in so doing stand with the many wives who also want to claim their voices in similar situations. All systems need to encourage the use of open, legitimate power.

We can help one another in the process of finding our own legitimate beneficent power. There is no power shortage; we can accept our own power while simultaneously working with others who accept and express theirs. Once we are in relationships that are mutually reciprocal, we realize what a burden it was to live otherwise.

Reevaluating the Concept of God's Power

Even our relationship with God is one of reciprocity, of shared power. God does not have all the power while we have none. We share the creative power of the universe and depend on one another for the evolving of the good. God can be thought of as a Spokesperson God, speaking (and hearing) from the stand of Love. God has the capacity to respond to our initiatives, to persuade us, but not to coerce us. When we think of ourselves made in the image and likeness of this Deity, we can see that we are emboldened to be spokespeople, with strong stands and with the capacity to implement much good in our relationships.

God has been referred to in the Judeo-Christian tradition as the Word. There is a sense in which we do identify God with the Word of Wisdom, that which is given to humans from beyond. Yet God is equally the Ear of the universe, hearing us into speech.[5] God breathes into us and gives us life. God also waits for our response, our speech, our giving of breath back to others and to God.

When we think of God as Spokesperson, standing boldly for love and peace and, as Ear of the universe, hearing our speech, we find we must shed the notion that God is all-powerful. God has the most power in the universe, and God's power is unrivaled, but God cannot force us to accept God's will. God's love and guidance are offered; they are spoken. It is up to us to respond. Our speaking up on behalf of others and our own values is part of our response.

Ultimately it is God who empowers us, yet I imagine playfully that God is worn out trying to persuade some of us to accept the power God is seeking to give us. It is up to us to accept our God-given capacity to implement.

Here are a variety of ways in which you can work to improve your own expression of beneficent power.

Notice how you participate in events and whom you expect to take charge, to have control. If you are a member of a group, complaining about how the group is functioning but assuming that someone else should take charge to make changes, you are shying away from your own power. Simply observing what is happening—that you are expecting other people to use their power to implement good for the group—can be empowering, *if* you take the next step: that is, take responsibility for your own action in the group by voicing your views.

You can take this observational stance in a one-to-one relationship as well. If you see yourself expecting the other person to say what he or she wants in order to discover your own wants, you can stop yourself in the process. You can insist to yourself that you find out *your* wants or opinions before you hear those of the other person.

"Do you want to go fishing next weekend with the Allans? They just called to ask us." You can stop yourself from immediately answering, "What do you want?" Give yourself time to discover your tentative decision. Then discuss each of your opinions. When you have become clearer regarding your opinion, your partner benefits from not having to guess what you really want. You can, of course, change your mind, because you see the situation differently after hearing your partner's opinion or because you are going to do what the other wants; someone has to compromise. But you will at least determine your opinion and know what you are doing.

Don't blame yourself for failing to communicate, when you have tried but the system in which you speak is unwilling to hear you. If something doesn't go right, don't blame yourself. Keep working, get help, but never leave the situation with the resignation that that's just the way things are. If one door is closed, one approach to speech, there is another door. You may run out of patience or energy to deal with a particular situation, but you can never run out of different ways to say things to someone.

The issue of gaining internal power is not one for individuals to deal with alone. We as a society orient family, work, and political systems around some people having more institutional power than others. Even when we as individuals do all we can to face and work through our own internal barriers to speaking with clarity, external barriers such as racism or sexism continue to haunt us. If each person in a family or community is aided to find her or his voice and given permission to speak, the system itself will undergo a realignment of power. If we seek to have healthier relationships in our systems, we will be changing those very systems.

It is not easy for people to keep asserting that they have the capacity to implement their lives according to their values and longings when other people and systems handicap their expression. Examples of this phenomenon abound. I, like most whites, am far too oblivious to many of the situations my colorful sisters and brothers face. However, occasionally I witness an event that reawakens me.

One such event occurred as I hailed a cab to go home from the Dayton airport. The African-American driver had just had an encounter with a white police officer. The driver did not know it was an off-duty officer when he pointed out calmly that the white man was backing up into the taxi loading zone. The officer resented having the taxi driver correct his actions, so he pulled back his jacket to expose his gun—a symbol of power and a statement more potent than words. The driver was stunned and angry at this misuse of institutional power.

These events could have occurred between a white police officer and a white taxi driver; however, a confrontation like this one is especially likely to place the African American in a quandary with regard to personal power precisely because he or she has already had to deal with it a number of times. The driver was still shaking when I got into the cab. (I was upset for him, too.) He told me he was a grown man; no one was going to treat him that way. He was embarrassed at feeling reduced and was trying to regain stature in his own eyes. For the twenty-minute ride home, I witnessed how he drew on his internal resources to reclaim his sense of power.

When he dropped me off at my corner, children were getting off the school bus, and we were both moved by the joyful, natural way in which the black and white children were chasing and laughing with one another. The driver and I had not mentioned color during our ride, but each of us knew it played a major role in both the incident and the driver's work to recoup his sense of self. He commented, as I gathered my suitcase, "Maybe there's hope for the future."

Reflecting often on this incident, I realized that part of his healing, and the release of any personal blame, was accomplished by regaining personal hope for himself in the future and by envisioning a future for his offspring in which internal power and self-esteem are firm precisely because the environment is also affirming.

Today some people who are invested with power because of the role they play do sincerely want to listen to all voices. A husband may want his wife to have equal power in their relationship and may wish to hear his wife's words clearly. An employer may want to hear the opinions and ideas of the employees. Those who are now wanting to hear may be puzzled and frustrated; the ones who had not spoken much before do not necessarily become talkative as soon as they are given the chance. It takes time to gather the power to speak and the trust that one will be heard.

If you have had your voice muted in the past, you may need to work extra hard to speak up, to take stands, for you are less acquainted with your own power and less trusting of the system's acceptance of your use of power. Don't blame yourself if you have difficulty speaking, if you take a good deal of time to express yourself, or if those with more institutional power are impatient and still have problems listening to you.

Accept the fact that you may not be fully understood when you speak. There appears to be safety in silence. At least no one can misunderstand your words. But with further thought we realize that even silence is often misunderstood. Silence is frequently taken for assent, when agreement was not intended. Others could misunderstand silence by thinking that you show lack of interest, when you really are interested, or that you are knowledgeable, when you know nothing about the subject. Silence is not safe after all, for others do not know you or your longings and values when you are silent.

When you speak, others do learn to know you and your opinions. But here there is risk, too, for your words can be misunderstood. Try as you may, you cannot guarantee that others will grasp your meaning completely. Their own prejudices and views, including their notions about what you are likely to say, get in the way of their hearing you. It takes much clarification to move through these barriers.

Let us say that you have been known in a particular setting as one who asks that children be included in the activities. When a dinner is planned, you ask what will be served to the children. When there is a speaker for an occasion, you inquire about baby-sitting provisions. Now the group is discussing an art project. You have an idea that is for the adults, and you are willing on this occasion to have an adults-only event. When you speak up with your idea, others may so expect that you *always* want children to be present that they may not be able to hear, until you explain for a third or fourth time that you are not always glued to intergenerational events.

With one-to-one long-term relationships the interactions are repeated so often that a huge buildup of expectations develops. When one person makes a real change, it may take considerable lag time for the other to hear the change.

It is not necessarily a failure of our speaking when we are misunderstood. If we are misunderstood frequently, we would be wise to look at ourselves to see whether we are camouflaging our meanings or being ambiguous. But we can be clear and honest, and another may still not understand us. The beauty of speech is that we can try again.

Repeat an encouraging phrase to yourself. In the children's story *The Little Engine That Could,* some of the engines that were asked to help answered that they were too important, too tired, or too busy. Then along came the Little Blue Engine, who had never climbed the mountain before but was willing to try. As she mounted higher and higher, she repeated, "I think I can, I think I can."

Some of us may feel like this engine when we try speaking up clearly and compassionately. We can be helped by having a phrase to repeat to ourselves whenever we need encouragement.

You will need to reflect to find a phrase that fits your situation and beliefs about God and yourself. The following are samples of sentences that could help you feel empowered to speak and keep speaking.

"God is with me as I speak."
"I am loved and loving as I speak."
"I can speak and be heard."
"I am heard by God and can be heard by [name]."

A husband feels desperate about needing more time with his wife. He has tried a variety of ways of communicating this need to her. At first he suggested going out regularly, but his wife tended to have something else to do on the planned evenings out. His next step was to talk to her directly, to explain that he felt their closeness slipping away, that he needed to be with her more. She seemed to hear his words, but she continued to be as evasive as ever. He tried acting paradoxically; he went places alone, trying to enjoy the solitude. He thought that he might learn to enjoy being alone—or that she might want to be with him—if he weren't so insistent about being with her. Now he wants to tell her once again that he is desperately lonely in the relationship. But he is afraid, for none of his earlier attempts seemed to make a dent in the situation. So, in preparing to speak to his wife, he says to himself again and again, "The Ear of God hears and guides me, no matter what."

This man may be in a situation where his wife simply will not respond to his needs. But his prayer phrase helps him have the courage to try again and face the consequences of his actions.

Act "as if" you have power. Many people think they have to *feel* power before they can *act* powerfully, but feelings, thoughts, and behaviors are all intertwined; each affects the other, and a change in any of the three affects the other two. If I think I am powerful, I begin to feel and act more powerful. Likewise, if I act more powerful, I begin to think of myself and feel myself to be powerful.

We can act "as if" we have power, even if we do not yet feel powerful. This is not to suggest that we be phony, but that we emphasize the confident part of ourselves, which is present to some degree, rather than focus on the part that is shaky.

I was unaccustomed to the power I had as a minister when I first officiated at weddings and funerals. The families who contacted me on these occasions expected me to be comfortable with my role. I found that I could act as if I were confident, as if I had appropriate power (capacity to implement) for the task. Not only was I empowering myself, I was also helping the families to be calm and assured.

I would not encourage anyone to repress or deny feelings. Acting "as if" is not a way to be rid of uncomfortable feelings by pretending they are not there. But in many cases we have a variety of feelings: We are fairly confident, a little afraid, a bit impatient. Acting as if we have the capacity to implement in a situation is a conscious choice to go with the preferred feelings for the sake of the action itself.

Write out the message. If we are stuck, having tried a variety of ways to communicate, or if we are too vulnerable or frightened to speak directly to a person or group, we can write out our message. We have a good deal of control of our language when we write; we do not need to worry whether or not our words will come out right. Writing is not as intimate as talking directly, but it is a viable choice—certainly better than avoiding the issue.

Not long ago some members of a committee prepared a proposal that concerned me greatly. I was so emotionally attached to the issues involved that I was afraid of being very nervous and shaky at the next meeting. I knew I could not remain silent, yet I knew a week in advance that I would be very uncomfortable during the next meeting when we debated the issue. So I chose to prepare a written response. While I was as calm as I could be at home, I wrote out my thoughts and feelings.

When the time for the meeting arrived I was still a little nervous, but since all present could read my response, I did not have to be anxious about what to say. I would not choose to write out many responses, but on this one occasion I needed to do it.

Couples occasionally find that writing notes to each other to clarify their positions is helpful. Sometimes an argument is almost over, but there are dangling unfinished items. A note that is written privately before it is shared can help both partners to hear and see straight. I think that a consistent use of written communications rather than a spontaneous flow of oral communications would be cumbersome and probably distancing in a relationship, but an occasional use of the pen provides emphasis and a surer way of saying what is meant.

Practice an empowerment exercise. Many exercises are designed to help us mobilize internal resources.[6] The following is an example.

Divide a paper into quarters. In the top left quadrant draw a picture or write words that occur to you as you ask yourself the question, "Where am I now in my life?" The picture can be symbolic or realistic. Next, in the top right square, draw a picture or write words that are in response to the question, "What is emerging in my life now?" In the bottom left quadrant, respond to "What is getting in my way?" and, in the last quarter, "What do I need to develop in order to take my next step? That is, what resources do I have that can be strengthened?"[7]

If you do this exercise, you may discover more clearly what is getting in your way of speaking or acting and, more importantly, you may remind yourself of the vital resources you possess.

The minister of education at a Korean church led her youth group in this exercise. She found that while the teenagers had seldom verbalized particular issues and feelings at their meetings, on this occasion they shared many important thoughts and feelings. They were empowered to speak by drawing first. Then they put into words what they had expressed on paper.

Ask to be heard until you are finished. If others do not give you adequate time to finish your speaking or if they interrupt you in mid-sentence, you have the right to ask to be heard until you are finished. You may have to ask many times before the habitual way of speaking with interruptions is altered, but with persistence you are likely to be heard.

My son learned from his preschool teachers to say, when interrupted, "Excuse me, please, I was talking." Our family was a bit surprised the first time he said this at home, but it surely was effective. His is the smallest voice at the dinner table, but with assertion on his part he could claim his rights. The teachers empowered him to use words to get his words heard.

A husband may say to his wife, "I want to know your opinion," and sincerely mean it. But if throughout her life she has had trouble finishing her sentences, doubting that her sentences would be heard or valued (because at one time they were not), she may not be able to respond instantly to her husband's genuine offer.

Don't worry about having to be right. One of the reasons people do not speak up is that they feel a pressure to be right. They are immobilized at times because they are unwilling to reveal their uncertainties or vulnerabilities.

We have to face uncertainty in our own positions if we are to be open to novelty. Rather than believing the popular stereotype that changing one's mind is a sign of weakness, we must understand that taking on new opinions is an outgrowth of learning new facts or seeing from a wider vantage point.

Persons in positions of authority often fear losing some of their authority if they change their minds. They may cling tenaciously to their decisions even when advisers suggest otherwise. It would be healthier for all concerned if they could accept the fact that they might change their minds. If these authority figures could experience the strength it takes to admit errors or changes of mind, they could speak in dialogue with others rather than issue edicts which, no matter how wrong they are, must be obeyed.

Be willing to borrow power. In our culture it is the middle generation that has authority in both family structures and institutional settings. The youthful and elder generations need to be heard, yet, precisely because of their life-stage concerns, both generations may need to *borrow* some authority occasionally. A grandmother may need to have her daughter or teenage grandson accompany her to the bank or the doctor's office in order to help her to be heard by the professionals who rush through their tasks too quickly for the grandmother to get in a word.

The teenage granddaughter may need to use the internal voice of her father or grandmother as she speaks up to her peers with her values. "My grandmother would be disappointed if I drank as a minor," or "I take piano lessons because my father wants me to." She may want to continue with the lessons and prefers not to drink because of her own values, but borrowing someone else's authority helps her speak until her internal voice becomes stronger.

For Reflection and Action

1. Think about how much "capacity to implement" (power) you feel that you have in your various relationships. Are there ways in which you can foster more reciprocal sharing of power?

2. Consider how you believe God's power acts in the world. How do you think human power interacts with God's power?

3. Look through the suggestions for empowering yourself and see which of them are applicable to you. Choose two suggestions to focus on in the next few days.

5

When and How to Speak

If only we could know how another will respond before we speak up with what we want to say. If only we could know our spouse's reaction to our expression of feelings. If only we could know the short-term and long-term effects our stand regarding attendance at church will have on our children. If only we could know how our boss will answer before we stand up for getting the full vacation that was promised to us.

There is a range of possibilities regarding this "if only" issue. At one end is the person who engages in endless rehearsals, imagining again and again how others will respond. At the other end is the one who blurts out whatever she or he wants, without any thought about how such behavior affects others.

Most people who are reading this book are probably somewhere in the middle, wanting to speak but aware that they cannot know or rehearse the response to the point of certainty. The time comes when we must speak, even though we don't know the effect it will have on others.

Once we know what we want to say, we have to decide when and how to say it. We cannot determine in advance how another will respond, yet we should give some consideration to the potential effect our speaking may have. For example, unless it is an emergency, it simply is not kind to raise a long-term child-

rearing issue with our spouse as she or he gets off the
airplane from a stressful trip. If we trust the process of
speaking, we can speak caringly and respectfully to
others without knowing the outcome.

**Persistent feelings should be shared; with fleeting
ones, be cautious.** In the sixties there was a trend in
small-group counseling that was heard by many as encouraging honest speech expressed spontaneously. "If I
feel something, it is appropriate to say it" seemed to be
the message. One of the contributors to this ethos, Carl
Rogers, said consistently in his writings during that
time that we should share persistent feelings; he did not
advise sharing every feeling that occurred.[1] An impulse
of anger may seem strong, but three hours later you
may have a genuinely difficult time remembering what
you were angry about. Waiting to share the anger only
if it is persistent can be prudent.

Some of us think very little about whether to talk—
anything inside us is made visible to others instantly. By
far the greatest error for many of us, though, is not
expressing something that *is* persistent. We have felt
anger for three months but cannot bring ourselves to
name the problem. We have wanted to ask for something for weeks, but wonder what would happen if we
did. For all of us, whether we are inclined to talk too
fast, without reflection, or to hold our breath when we
are preoccupied with a concern, the guideline to share
when the concern is *persistent* is useful.

Use empathy as a bridge to others. Second-guessing
what the other will say has the implication of trying to
figure out how the other will respond in order to get the
best for ourselves. That really is not useful in the process of speaking up. First of all, it is nearly impossible,

and second, it is entirely self-serving—trying to stack things to benefit ourselves.

Seeking to have empathy for the others to whom we want to speak is valuable for both the hearer and the speaker. Empathy is trying to stand in the other's shoes. It is thinking imaginatively of the life of the other, trying to grasp that person's feelings, her or his life experiences and current state.

Your daughter's boyfriend seems irresponsible to you, so you want to make clear to her your stand regarding dating. But your daughter has a chemistry exam tomorrow morning. A small dose of empathy leads you to see that now is not a good time to discuss the matter. You can, however, determine that you are going to speak to her tomorrow evening, thereby freeing yourself from the gnawing concern about whether or not to speak.

Empathy is essential for sharing preferences about the expression of sexuality while a couple is having intercourse. "Honey, this feels really good, but that hurts a little," is acceptable and probably will be heard as a loving response to a caring intent. Yet some couples have much difficulty mentioning their feelings or responses while they are actually physically close to each other. The solution is not to remain quiet and create further tension. Those couples can choose another time, while they are not making love, to discuss their preferences.

It is clear from these few examples that having empathy for another affects the timing of our sharing. It is not so much that we wait until our spouse or friend is well fed and content to bring something up that is important, as it is that we try to consider when and how the other can hear the message as we intend it, without interferences from his or her own preoccupations. It is

not helpful to become *preoccupied* with finding a time
to talk, but giving thought to the timing is likely to be
productive and kind.

One way we can communicate empathy is to announce our expectation about how the hearer will feel
when he or she hears our statement. For example, a
teacher may say, "I expect that you will be disappointed, but you failed the test." Another way to share
some consideration for the possible effect of our comment is to state our own experience as we speak. The
same teacher could say, "I am sorry to tell you this, but
you did fail the test." If we cushioned everything we
said, we would sound ridiculous, but some acknowledg-
ment of the anticipatory feelings of the hearer will make
for a clearer understanding that we care.

Holding breath, withholding speech, avoids community. Holding breath, withholding speech, leads to
privatistic individuals isolating themselves from one another—"polite" but never intimate or deeply caring.
Giving breath risks big open meetings—all talking together in one place. Giving breath trusts community.

**Loosen creativity by taking a wise pause to find three
options.** One way to make decisions about when and
how to speak is to think of three options that are available while we are in the midst of an occasion.[2] The
advice to find three options before acting on one is
useful in many settings. I often tell ministry students
that they should have three options in mind of what to
do or say while they counsel. As long as they are wed-
ded to only one type of response, they are acting habitu-
ally, not with depth of forethought or fresh wisdom.

When we sit in an audience disagreeing with a
speaker, we can easily feel caught in an either-or bind:
Either we speak up or we remain quiet. Clearly it is my
bias that far too many people remain quiet when all

would benefit if they spoke. But speaking up may not mean that we *have* to talk in front of the whole group; there are other alternatives. We could write a note to the speaker, stay for a talk after the program, discuss the concern with the people who are responsible for the event, or speak through our behavior by leaving the lecture. Our choice of action is highly dependent on the context. The various ways of speaking that are not public will not directly communicate to the whole audience, and walking out is not easily interpreted. But if we manage to remind ourselves that we have at least three options, we would give ourselves more freedom to choose before acting.

Thinking of three choices is a way that an individual can pry himself or herself free from an apparent either-or predicament. But it can also be useful with two people or a whole family or group. A family of five (with three older teenagers) was trying to decide how to make their limited amount of money go around for Christmas gifts. At first it seemed to one parent that there was only one solution: Divide all the money into five portions, so that each could have an equal amount of money to buy presents. One of the teenagers thought the decision was an either-or predicament: Either the adults have money to buy presents for the teenagers or the teenagers have money to buy presents for the parents.

If the whole family decided to try the three-choice option, each member would privately think of three possibilities. Then each would share his or her three options. Ideas may emerge, such as: give most of the money to some concern we all care about, using the rest to make a really exciting Christmas dinner we all cook; find odd jobs for the teenagers in the neighborhood so that they can have more money; draw names so that each person gives only one other person a present; agree

that every person is going to make presents this year;
wait until February to share presents, since there won't
be such a money crunch at that time; each bring a story
about how Christmas is celebrated by some other family; work together to create a Christmas play the whole
family can put on for friends.

Since each member has to present three options, no
one person will have presented the option that is chosen
without also presenting two options that were dis-
carded. In presenting all the options, there is not as
much attachment to "my" solution. After all the ideas
are presented, there is a sense of amazement that there
could be so many ideas from what seemed to be such
a stalled situation.

The three-choice exercise is really a way of pushing
the imagination to work. Too often we fall into thinking
that God wills things to happen. That gets us stuck in
a mode of discerning what *one* thing is right. But we
can also think of God as imagining many things for us.
Perhaps God has no right answer for the family at
Christmastime. God simply wants each member of the
family and the family as a whole to experience anew the
birth of God's love, which can be known through
Christ. God might be imagining how transformation
and new birth can take place in the family *while* the
family is using their imagination to find solutions.

To loosen creativity is an exciting adventure. I like to
think of Jesus as stopping to loosen creativity when he
paused, wrote something in the sand, and then ad-
dressed the crowd that was about to stone the woman
who was caught in adultery. I call what he did taking
a "wise pause." He took time when people tried to
corner him. During that time his imagination was enabling him to find the creative solution he finally chose.
(His solution was to reframe the issue, asking who
among all those gathered could throw the first stone.)

Willpower so often implies that we must force ourselves to do that which we would really not like to do. Imagination is a gift of the spirit that is more like God's way of acting. It is the envisioning of possibilities.

Announce the level of importance of the message in advance. Our messages may sound the same but have very different levels of importance. It is helpful to communicate not only the message but also its importance. One way of thinking of the levels is to consider that some things we say are just opinions or preferences (level one), others are concerns about the person to whom we speak (level two), while still others are about the relationship itself (level three).

A husband can say, "You know, this is just a preference, but I really do like it when you put away your clothes." The wife can hear this at the level it is intended—just a preference, level one. She can respond by adapting to meet his preference if putting away her clothes is not too difficult for her. Perhaps she never knew that leaving clothes around the house was of any concern to her husband; now she does, so she tries harder to pick up after herself.

But perhaps this is not just a minor issue for the husband; perhaps he is really getting irritated by what he perceives as her constant messiness. He is beginning to think of her as a lazy person. Speaking truthfully, he gives a clear level-two message, "It may seem like very little to you or a lot, I don't know. But I am really bugged by these clothes around the house. I begin to think of you as messy. This is really getting to me."

If he is so upset by the clothes around the house that he doubts being able to continue living with his wife, he had better communicate the importance of his concern, for it has reached level three. He needs to say, "I cannot live in these conditions. We have to find a solution quickly, because I'm at my wits' end. This is affecting our relationship."

The levels may sound silly over such an issue as clothes, yet there are times when two people talk but have very different perceptions of the level of importance. We cannot expect the other to know how important something is to us. He may make a mountain out of a molehill. But if he does hear my molehill as a mountain, that may be partly my fault for not communicating clearly in the first place that it is just a molehill but worth discussing. Likewise, she may just dismiss something that matters so much to me, in large part because she does not realize how much it matters.

Couples have reported to me that they began announcing during their discussions, "This is a level-two concern." The humor that was thus introduced added creativity to the clarity provided by the level-sharing.

Try to have enough time, though you can't always wait for that. Parents of young children may seldom have a moment to themselves, without hearing "Mommy!" or "Daddy!" from the next room or feeling little hands tugging for attention. By the time parents are finally alone and the children asleep, the time is so precious that each may hesitate to speak up with a concern or longing. Talking may prolong the day and diminish even more the little sleep available. Parents of teenagers may find they have no privacy, for the children stay up later than the parents do.

There is no doubt that talking clearly, to communicate one's stands intentionally and lovingly, takes time. At some point the talking itself has to become a priority in the relationship. Consider the value of checkups and regular vaccinations at the doctor's and dentist's offices. We see that though they cost time and money, they prevent much greater expenditures and pain in the future. Likewise, speaking to one another is a checkup and a means of preventing pain in the future. Speaking is a way of nurturing the relationship. It is worth the time it takes.

When we speak with a friend, we do not need to arrive at conclusions within one conversation. We may be more willing to take time if we expect that the discussion will be an installment in the midst of an ongoing communication. The aim is movement and understanding. Friends surely can spend a little time reflecting on something about which one of them wants to speak. In this way the one who wants to initiate speaking is not being held in abeyance altogether.

Be aware that families thrive on consistency; they will often resist change. Speaking introduces change. Change can improve families, but family members may not see it that way at first.

Families and systems of people hold even more tenaciously to their past purposes than individuals do. Imperceptibly and usually without planning, family systems create the pattern by which they function. Roles and tasks are gradually adopted. Each person has some security in maintaining his or her role, identity, and purpose in the greater system (even if there is pain attached to that position). If one person decides to make a change in her or his behavior or attitudes, the other members may deliberately or inadvertently hinder that change. Even when it is to the advantage of the other members for the change to occur, it takes work and energy and incurs some fear of loss on their part.

One member usually decides to speak up precisely when that person has decided to break the status quo, either to ask the system to look at itself or to ask the system to change to meet this person's (or another's) needs. No one person in any system can change without

affecting everyone else. If one parent decides, "I want
to go out to the movies; I'm tired of just seeing them
on the VCR," that is not just a personal stand. A baby-
sitter must be found. The children will have positive
and negative responses to the effects on them. Or, in
another family, if a teenager is no longer the "silent
one" in the family, the sibling who has been called "Ms.
Talkative" will have to readjust her perception not only
of her sibling but also of herself.

Systems resist change even more than people do, but
I believe that God encourages groups of people to enter-
tain novel ideas and creative solutions just as God per-
suades individuals to appreciate growth. God can
envisage how each member can find creative growth
and at the same time see how the family can grow as
a family.

A couple are excited when they marry. Both start to
work outside the home, and both of them are vitally
interested in their jobs. But the husband becomes re-
flective when his father dies and decides he wants more
leisure time with his wife. He wants more intensity in
their relationship in terms of diverse activities shared
together. For the couple to accept the introduction of
greater intensity in their relationship requires a willingness to let go of some of the private investments each
has made in her or his work. They may even have to
destroy or modify some of their private dreams. If they
completely avoid the man's longings, the relationship
may yield what this husband would experience as trivi-
ality—his job and occasional meals and sex together
with his wife are not enough. They have to bring into
balance again and again through the years of their marriage their private and collective longings. Each time
one speaks up for change, a new balance needs to be
renegotiated.

For Reflection and Action

1. Think about some feeling or idea you would like to express to someone. Consider it from a variety of perspectives: How persistent is the feeling or idea? How is the person (or people) to whom you want to speak likely to feel on hearing you? What are three options for your choice of actions at this point? Exactly how important is your comment (which of the three levels)? How can you make time to speak? What effect would your voice have on the whole system?

2. Consider a time when you feel that you missed an opportunity to speak by remaining silent. Think of how you might have spoken and when, considering possible outcomes (both short-term and long-term).

3. Recall a time when you spoke up and were amazed with the beneficial results for individuals or the community. What happened that made it work so well?

6

Empowering Others to Speak

A little girl starting kindergarten faces many new experiences. She is scared because the driver stops the bus in the middle of the intersection; she is baffled as to how to stay out of trouble when others talk to her during quiet time. So she asks her mother to talk to the bus driver and the teacher for her. The bus driver explains to the mother that he goes into the intersection to prevent cars from passing the bus, and the teacher suggests a solution to the quiet-time dilemma. This is a crucial moment. The parents do need to help the kindergartner become comfortable with school, and some speaking for the girl is a bridge toward that acclimatization. However, the parents need to tell the girl how to speak for herself. The next time there is a question at school, the girl must be encouraged to ask the teacher about it herself. Surely there will be other times when the parents do the speaking, but they are not helping their daughter if they continue to speak for her most of the time.

Sometimes we unwittingly become involved in a family or office or friendship system similar to the one created by the kindergartner, the parents, and the school personnel. Your friend talks to *you* about a problem instead of the person he needs to address. How do you enable him to speak for himself?

Most important, you can say that you think it is of

little use to tell you the situation. He needs to talk directly to the person with whom he has the problem.

If he is reluctant to speak directly, given your encouragement, you can offer a few other suggestions. You can mention that he could write out what he would like to say to the person. You could even read his written message and explore the implications with him. With your assurance that the written words are all right, he might more confidently give it to the person or speak to the person without the notes.

You could explore with him the timing for a conversation with the person. For example, he might decide on a time by which he will have spoken or a situation in which the speaking could be done.

If he is willing to reflect seriously with you, you can suggest that he role-play discussing the concern. Ask him to speak to the person in his imagination, to talk out loud. It is often helpful to get an empty chair that represents the person. He says to the chair what he really wants to say to the person. Then you suggest that he sit in the chair and respond to his own comments as the other person. He might carry on a dialogue in this fashion. (It is best if you do not play the role of the other, but rather have him speak to the chair that represents the person.)

If you have been consistent in saying that the only way for him to solve his problem is for him to speak to the other person, and if he has found ways to resist all your recommendations, it may be best to refuse to listen any more to talk about that situation. This may sound uncaring, but it may be the most caring action you can take. He is avoiding talking, using you to keep avoiding action where it should be taken. If you frustrate his avoidance, he will have to do something else. You can be clear that you still care, that you are willing to talk about other things, but you believe he is avoiding dealing with the person he must talk to by talking to you instead. You can communicate that you think you are perpetuating the problem by continuing your conversation about the issue. Out of concern for the outcome, you are withdrawing yourself from being part of the problem.

To enable people to speak for themselves is an enormous gift. We are saying that we believe they have the power and insight to take care of themselves. There are ample opportunities to offer long-term preparation for the empowerment of others.

Restrain your own speech. If you, because of your role, have more power in the system (family, work, church), restrain your own speech in order to give others the time and opportunity to speak. Often those who have more power need to withdraw their voices consistently and long enough for others to grasp that they, too, really will be heard.

I experienced this phenomenon in relation to my children one week when I had laryngitis. I had been accustomed to reading to them before they went to bed. However, since I could not speak, they decided to read to me. That delightful switch began what is now a shared reading time.

Each of us has experienced a time when someone was trying to teach us something—to bake cookies, to find a place on a map, to learn a computer game, to memorize a poem. As long as the "teacher" kept doing the actions or the speaking, our learning was minimal. It was only after the teacher said, "Here, you try it," that we really grasped the skill or knowledge.

Sometimes a person in authority can refer someone to another person, thereby empowering both the person with the request and the one to whom the referral is made. My pediatrician strongly values breast-feeding;

that was one reason I chose him before our children were born. When I was having difficulty, he referred me to a nurse at a nearby hospital who is an expert in the field.

One visit with the nurse, and I was empowered in my nursing capacities. My doctor did not need to take charge, acting as if he were an expert on nursing. His actions communicated that he trusted women as resources for each other.

There are many instances in which we can empower others by not taking on requests of us as mandatory requirements for our answers. "Mom or Dad, please do this homework; it's too hard for me," certainly should not be a trigger for the parents to give the answers (if they can). Rather, it is an invitation for wrestling with the subject together. When counselors are asked for help, they know that it is rarely best just to give their ideas of what to do. The clients may want answers, but the clients are *empowered* by being enabled to find their own answers, for then they can continue to find their own answers as other issues arise.

Share facts as well as resources with those who have less institutional power. Ruth James is the name of a young migrant worker who was interviewed in a powerful chapter of the book *Women of Crisis* by Robert Coles. She says:

> That nurse who comes here and teaches us how to use pills or get fitted is the best friend we have. No wonder the crew leader wants to get rid of her and her program. He says she's an outsider, that nurse. He says she's white, and she doesn't understand us. But she understands all right—she understands him; that's what has him worried. He keeps asking me when I'm going to have a baby. He looks at me as if to say I'll never be a

real slave of his until I come up with that kid! Then I'll
be hooked! That's the one big lesson I've learned. I was
never good in school, and I never liked those people
who came to the camps and wanted to teach us and get
us "organized." But the nurse who gave us the story on
birth control, she was the biggest help of my life.[1]

Simply sharing facts with people who do not have
them is empowering. A girl can say that she does not
want to become pregnant and can enforce her words
if she knows how to take precautions. If she does not
know what precautions to take, she can hardly voice
her desires with any power. Education is empowering.
It is cruel to keep facts from people who are likely to
become enslaved by the lack of them.

Throughout the world, when people who had been
illiterate were taught to read, they were able to speak
up with more power in their communities and societies.
The acquiring of knowledge is empowering.

**Learn to recognize and appreciate that people speak
up in different manners.** People who tend to be intro-
verted are likely to process information silently for a
while before they share their conclusions or opinions.
They mull over ideas in their minds before they speak;
what is spoken is then clear and concise. Those who are
more extroverted tend to process information while
they talk. They mull over their ideas aloud, letting the
other person hear the processing as it occurs.

The introvert may think that the extrovert has not
been very decisive when she or he hears the tentative
ideas and indecisions that come with the statement.
Meanwhile, the extrovert may be impatient, having to
wait for the other to say something. In fact, the extrovert may interrupt before the introvert gets something

said. The latter will then begin processing the additional comments, taking even longer before saying something.

Power can be held by talking quickly to dominate the conversation (the extrovert's technique) or by preparing carefully phrased and finalized comments that seem unchallengeable (the introvert's method). Just knowing that the other person is different may provide enough patience and laughter to get the communication shared and the power equalized. Neither person needs to be like the other to make the relationship work.

Provide listening environments. A psychiatric nurse was asked to help with an exceptionally withdrawn man. A variety of other nurses and doctors had tried to help him but to no avail, since he simply would not speak. This nurse approached him, sat down, and said, "I'm from mental health. Your nurses tell me you are depressed." The next fifteen minutes were filled with nonstop talking by the patient. Finally the nurse commented, recalling that the others had told her he had not spoken. "You don't seem to have trouble talking about yourself." "Well," he replied, "you're different from all the other nurses—you sat down." The nurse had communicated nonverbally that she was with the man while he spoke. She cared about what he said and conveyed that openness.

The number-one way to empower another to speak is to listen. Theologian Nelle Morton cites diverse examples of people who were "heard into speech." Whether they were deaf persons, people in deep mourning, women who had not felt that they were heard, or children learning to talk, the people were immersed in an environment of one or more persons who stayed by them, quiet and encouraging—more eager to listen than to talk. These speakers did not know what they were going to say (in some cases they did not even know how to talk) until they were heard. We tend to think that speaking is first; hearing follows. Morton witnessed the fact again and again that much of the time hearing has to be guaranteed *before* speech is born.

The first time she saw this phenomenon, Morton was with a group of women as one of them sought to express herself. The speaker was quiet for a while; she made attempts to communicate as she tried to find what she wanted to say. Slowly, she managed to say *all* that she had to say. No one in the group interrupted her, rushed her, or tried to comfort her prematurely. Although it seemed to be a reversal of ordinary logic, it was clear that the hearing of the group enabled the woman to speak. They heard her into speech.[2]

Our son gave me the opportunity to witness this need to be heard into speech when he was a toddler. He refused to move on to his next words or sentences until I repeated what he had said. Most of the time the process was simple, for he would say something like, "Ball, over there, I want it." I would respond, "The ball is there; you want it," as I rolled it to him. Sometimes it was not so easy. When I did not understand what he had said, I would try saying, "Yes, mm-hmm," but that did not work, for he just repeated the sentence. I would try again to respond to his words. At times I became exasperated, trying to move the conversation along. I was amazed that he was so tenacious in his determination to be understood. I realized along the way that he was not just trying to get me to understand him but was also clarifying his own thoughts.

While people at every age need to be listened to, the toddler, the teenager, and the older person have life-stage tasks that make it even more important for them to have attentive listeners. Toddlers are practicing saying things. They are beginning to realize that they have the power to communicate as they gain autonomy in both the direction of speech and the direction of loco-motion. If they are interrupted or ignored too fre-quently, they may reduce their efforts to communicate.

Teenagers are questioning many things; they are ex-ploring what they stand for. They are finding their identity for their upcoming adulthood. They need to be allowed to talk about themselves, their faith, their opin-ions on politics, their views of the world.

Older persons have memories and hopes, but they probably have to accept many losses and limitations. As they lose some of the natural avenues of communica-tion with friends and mates, those who do relate need to realize how much they need to be heard.

Teenagers are often quiet when their parents desper-ately want them to talk. Older people, on the other hand, often fear talking too much to their middle-aged children. The middle generation can listen in both di-rections, but it is really best if the younger and the older generations have additional forums besides their nu-clear families in which to be heard. That is one reason youth groups and senior citizen groups are so valuable.

At the church where I served in San Diego, we had at least six members who were over ninety years old. To celebrate these folk and let them know that we still thought they had something worthwhile to say, we held a "Wise Nineties Night." These experienced people were given the opportunity to share their ideas, poems, or whatever else they wanted to communicate to their church friends and family members. It was quite an impressive evening.

Shortly after that evening, the youth group wanted to have equal time. We called that event "Youth Speaks Out." The ninety-year-olds had been stunned and grateful that we still cared to hear from them. The young people were skeptical that we adults really would listen and asked again and again before the event whether they could speak on any topic they wanted. They appreciated the opportunity to make their remarks and felt respected afterward.

Listen actively! No other interpersonal skill seems so simple but is so difficult to grasp as active empathic listening. Many people say, "I just listened." That "just" is inappropriate. When we listen *and communicate what we have heard,* we are empowering the speaker.

When I say active listening, I mean that we are attentive to the kinds of responses we give. It is possible to hear what a person said but for the person not to know that we heard. It is also possible that we hear, the speaker believes that we have heard, but, to the surprise of both of us, we have not understood.

It takes active listening to communicate back to the speaker what we think we have heard in order to see whether we have received the intended message. I appreciate the forty-year-old classification of E. H. Porter, who saw that verbal responses can fit into five categories: evaluative, interpretive, supportive, probing, and understanding.[3] (I refer to these responses as E,I,S,P, and U.) While each response is called for on some occasions, Porter's theory and much evidence in the past four decades have shown that a consistent use of understanding responses enables people both to be heard and to find their own answers to their problems.

Let us imagine that the woman next door approaches you, saying, "I'd like your help. I have been chosen to attend a year of additional training for my job. I'd get the same pay, but I'd have to do reading and written assignments at home after work. Then, of course, I'd be eligible for a promotion after that year. Sounds good, but I don't know if I'm up to it. What do you think?"

You can respond in a variety of ways: (1) "That sounds like a wonderful opportunity; of course you should take it." (2) "You doubt your capacities; you need to get over your sense of inferiority." (3) "I know you'll make the best decision; a few months from now you'll look back and wonder why you worried about it." (4) "What do your children and husband think? Have you done anything like this before?" (5) "You seem attracted to the opportunity, but you have some reservations about the extra work."

The first response is *evaluative;* it tells the neighbor what to do. Evaluative statements offer judgments of goodness, rightness, or appropriateness of action. This type of response is preferred by those who like to be experts or who are attached to "helping" people. Many people who ask for help, as this neighbor did, are relieved when you tell them what to do. She thinks she got what she wanted. But there is very often a letdown. The neighbor goes away muttering, "I've just been told I should say yes, but I'm not sure." If the neighbor takes the opportunity offered her, she is likely to feel a bit awkward, unsure whether she did it because you told her to or because it was her own decision. If the neighbor does not take the opportunity, she is likely to worry about what you will think of her for not taking your advice.

The second response ("You doubt your capacities; you need to get over your sense of inferiority") is *interpretive.* This is the response of an amateur psychologist who analyzes the situation, suggesting what the friend ought to think. Those who are inclined toward this response are bent on teaching others or showing them meanings. The neighbor could react in diverse ways to being interpreted, but none of them helps her make the decision herself. She feels in some way that she is not all right. You have suggested that you are a little more insightful than she.

Many caring people think that reassurance is the best thing to give to others who ask for help. After all, they think, I want to make them feel better. So these people respond with a third kind of response, comments such as "Don't worry" or "It'll be fine." In this case the responder answered, "I know you'll make the best decision." This is a *supportive* response, for it intends to pacify, to suggest in some way that the neighbor need not feel as she does. While it is certainly kind to be hopeful with others, this attempt at a reassuring response includes a hidden message that implies "I think you are wrong to worry" or "I don't want to be bothered with your useless worry." The one who asks for help is left not feeling heard. She *is* worried but is told she should not be.

The fourth possibility is to ask for more information—it is the *probing* response. This response puts the listener in the position of authority, suggesting that with enough information it would be possible to tell the neighbor what to do. Most of the time it is unnecessary to ask questions. Relevant information will emerge in the conversation.

Finally, the fifth response is the *understanding* one, the one that most empowers people to do their own speaking, to take their own initiatives. More than anything, this empathic response lets the inquirer know she was heard. In this case, the neighbor was heard in her interest *and* in her reluctance; both sides of the ambivalence were acknowledged by the listener. The listener refuses to be the authority on what the neighbor ought to *do* or what the neighbor should *think*. The listener, more than anything, is a mirror, reflecting what is heard, not in exactly the same words but with fresh words.

Responsive adults who care for infants act like a mirror—gooing in response to a goo, smiling with a smile, frowning with a frown. Even before the baby understands words as words, these adults are empowering the baby to speak. Mimicking dialogue gives the message that there already is a giving and receiving in the relationship, respect and expectation. This mirroring response done with infants is very similar to active listening for persons of any age.

We can see the value of empowering young children by our rudimentary understanding responses, yet we often forget to keep this up. Several mothers who learned how to listen actively realized that they had not been responding to their older children in this fashion. They had taken on the habit of responding with evaluative or supportive responses. These women decided to try understanding responses with intentionality for several weeks. They found remarkable consequences. Their children talked more and were less defensive about their mothers' comments, and the mothers felt more connected with the children, more respectful of the children's capacities.

Many people expect that understanding responses are never confrontations, but this is not so. Consider a mirror. The mirror shows you what you look like, gray hairs, pimples, frown, and all. The empathic response is a mirror—it reflects everything the speaker said, without filtering out the uncomfortable segments. Only the understanding response to the neighbor picked up the ambivalence, the reluctance to take the job training, as well as the gratefulness for the opportunity.

The important element of an understanding response is that you communicate what you have thought you heard. You may have heard something different from what the speaker meant, which is all right. Since you say what you heard, the speaker knows you have not heard what she intended, so she can then clarify her message. Sometimes you do hear what the speaker *said,* but when you mirror it back to her she realizes that is not really what she *meant.* The mirroring helps her discover what she does mean. It is this fine-tuning process that evokes answers from the speaker herself.

In our example you said, "You seem attracted to the opportunity, but you have some reservations about the extra work." The neighbor may hear that and realize that the work is not the concern. She may respond, "No, I'm not worried about the extra work as much as I am afraid of how my peers will react to my being chosen." Now you have more information (without having probed for it). The neighbor has clarified her dilemma for herself. Your hearing—and responding actively—enabled her to gain greater clarity. You can now respond, "You're excited, but you think that some of your co-workers will be jealous." You are again listening actively.[4]

Speaking as a chorus. I have emphasized the need to empower others to do their own speaking. Once another is empowered in this manner, that person has the gift for life. Certainly we benefit from our own capacity to implement, but we are not always in solo endeavors. In many situations we need a chorus of voices; lone voices are not sufficient.

Using the distinction I have made in this book, to be a Christian is not just a decision, it is a stand. Jews can say the same thing about Judaism. To be a Jew is integral to one's identity; it includes a stand-taking perspective. We need to realize that it means something to be a Christian or a Jew, or whatever religion we are. Genuine faith means that we stand for respect and peace among nations. We stand for helping our neighbors as responsible participants in the world. The impact of a religious body is more powerful precisely because it is a chorus. The carefully worded denominational statements on peace carry some weight to influence people. Equally important, the sense of being joined in a chorus to carry a particular refrain empowers us to keep on singing.

We sit simultaneously in a variety of choruses. At work, governing bodies discuss issues together and affect one another as they speak. It is tragic to have only the women speak up for concerns that would affect women, only people of color speak up for issues regarding people of color, only those with handicapping conditions speak up for others with similar physical conditions. Our presence with one another should remind us to speak up *for* one another.

Americans ought to speak up with Germans and other Europeans who ask for our missiles to be taken out of their countries. We should speak with them not only to help them but also because we realize that we are all in danger as long as the missiles are present.

Anyone who suspects that incest is taking place must speak up. Even if the one who has the suspicion (often the mother) feels powerless herself, she must realize that she has more power than the victim does. Even the perpetrator is suffering as he hurts another. They are in the system together, and all need help.

All speakers have blind spots, areas in which we do not see clearly beyond our personal viewpoints. We never "arrive" at a point where we can be sensitive to everyone, but if all of us keep speaking—and listening—we can all increase the perspectives from which we see and act. Queen Esther did not see that peace for her Jewish people *could* mean that no one—not even the "enemy"—gets massacred. She spoke for some people, but not for all people. Her focus, like that of most leaders, was to save her people. To see and take perspectives that are much larger than our own is a lifelong goal. It is a religious as well as a psychological task.

I believe that God is with each of us as we take our stands, both those we take at an unconscious level and those with which we wrestle consciously. I think of God as a Value Giver and Value Organizer for us. If we consciously attend to God in the process of stand taking, there is greater hope that we may make wise choices. However, I believe that God is involved in the process of our stand taking whether or not we think of God and whether or not we think about stand taking. That is, we cannot get God out of the process, but if we intentionally include God in the process, we may be more receptive to God's desires and weigh them more heavily in our speaking.

Prophets are attentive to their feelings as well as their reasoning and willing, for they know that God speaks through all our human dimensions. The Duke of Albany in *King Lear* is seldom thought of as a prophet, but he says what needs to be said in his context. He is still on stage at the end of the play, when many of the leaders have died. He is now in charge and could start giving orders to begin picking up the pieces. However, that would not be fitting to the occasion. There needs to be public mourning, the expression of feelings. In this context he says, "The weight of this sad time we must obey. Speak what we feel, not what we ought to say."[5]

Many times we follow a set of routine behaviors as we sit in a meeting or with our families. We think we ought to do our prescribed tasks according to our habitual patterns and roles. But if we do this, we act as Albany would have, had he disregarded his feelings and his grasp of the emotions of others. Yet we do this all the time! We push through a vote when we are not at all ready as a community to come to a decision. We end a family event with dangling feelings that are clearly begging for a little more time and attention. When we are attentive to the need to speak to and with a chorus, we can become compassionately passionate. We can speak, as Albany did, a word of catharsis, consolation, or challenge. Healing of persons and of families is promoted when we attend to our inner stirrings, pick up empathically the feelings of others, and speak what we discern needs to be said.

These prophetic words continue to echo in our ears precisely because they are passionate and are spoken by one who knows what to say: "The Spirit of the Lord is upon me, because he has anointed me to preach good news to the poor. He has sent me to proclaim release to the captives and recovering of sight to the blind, to set at liberty those who are oppressed, to proclaim the acceptable year of the Lord" (Luke 4:18–19).

For Reflection and Action

1. Notice how you respond to five people during one day. Using Porter's "E,I,S,P, and U" scheme, find whether you tend to evaluate, interpret, support, probe, or communicate understanding responses. If you have responded with options other than understanding ones, try to find an understanding option you could have offered.

2. Put yourself in the position of a person who is important to you (spouse, child, parent, friend) to consider how he or she experiences speaking up in several settings. Imagine how that person's position differs from yours, because of age, sex, or other circumstances.

3. Practice a daily discipline for a week in which you seek once a day to create a comfortable environment for another person to speak to you.

4. List the stands you have taken during the past year. (You may be able to identify stands you took as

you remember events in your family, with your friends, in your community, at church, at work, etc.) Now choose any other year in your life and do the best you can to recollect stands you took that year. Compare the two lists to see how you and your circumstances have changed.

7

Giving and Receiving Speech

When we speak up in our personal relationships, we can achieve personal integrity and greater intimacy. Integrity is the result of being congruent—matching our actions with our stands. Greater intimacy ensues as we give and receive words honestly spoken.

An eighty-nine-year-old woman demonstrated extraordinary integrity through her speaking during the last few months of her best friend's life. The woman with whom she had lived for over sixty years became ill and was taken to the hospital. When the friend had recuperated enough to leave the hospital, this woman assumed that she would take her home, but the people at the hospital said she should go to a nursing home. When the woman asked what would be needed to take her friend back to her own home, she was told that the friend would have to have live-in nursing care. Within eighteen hours this woman arranged the live-in care, but the doctor still considered it unwise for the friend to go home. She was taken to a nursing home and died within three weeks.

The woman said she had been haunted by memories of those three weeks; she wished she could have done more to get her friend home. She did not get what she asked for, but she truly had done all she could. She had known her stand; she had articulated it with as much voice as she had. The doctor's power was greater than hers in that situation, but she had remained true to her integrity, and that helped her to move through her grief with self-acceptance.

Learning to take stands is a lifelong task. Even when we think we are clear about our values and willing to speak them, we sometimes find ourselves in situations in which our stands conflict. Carl is a farmer who, after experiencing conflict between two values, told a colleague of mine that sometimes it is easier not to take a stand. This was not characteristic of him, for he saw himself as a stand taker for sound agricultural practices; he was adamantly against using chemical pesticides and farmed his own acres without them.

What prompted the comment to my colleague was a recent encounter he had had with his brother, who was also a farmer. When Carl learned that his brother needed help, he went over to his farm. His brother did use pesticides, and although he knew Carl was against them, when Carl arrived and asked what he could do first, the brother pointed to the pesticides, saying that spraying would probably be the best next step. Carl said nothing; he chose to help his brother put pesticides on his farm.

Carl thought of this as not taking a stand. Although he did not call it one, I would say that not arguing with his brother was a stand. His conflict was between two stands: not arguing with his brother and not using pesticides. He did not find a way on the spur of the moment to integrate the stands, so he chose one over the other. Of course, with further reflection and time, he might have decided to tell his brother his dilemma, to talk out his concerns. For instance, he could have said that he genuinely wanted to help but that he had a hard time doing something that was against his values. He could have asked to help with another task instead.

Carl, a stand taker, is still growing in his capacity to

implement and integrate his values. He can try to bring together his care for his brother and his concern for health by explaining why he has changed his agricultural practices and why his brother should do the same. All of us grow as we risk revealing our thoughts and feelings with others. We can move away barriers, becoming more honest and intimate.

Throughout this book we have seen the importance of befriending conflict, understanding our unconscious values, and using our internal power. We have learned the importance of grasping other perspectives to gain empathy and have explored ways to empower others to speak. To achieve clear speaking and hearing in relationships takes work. We have many concrete ways to reach our goal.

It may seem that speaking up, taking a stand, is a serious endeavor. You may have visions of yourself becoming aggressive or quick to anger. You may fear that, if you attend too much to stand taking, you may become dour or narrowly focused. It does not need to be that way.

Emma Goldman, an anarchist and revolutionary leader at the beginning of this century, took strong stands as she campaigned for justice in the world. In response to the humorlessness of some of her fellow activists, she said, "If I can't dance at your revolution, I don't want to come." We can dance as we relate to each other; we can dance as we stand and speak.

We can have confidence in our dancing because we trust that God is with us. Martin Luther King, Jr., gives a potent description of how he experienced God to be with him.

In this state of exhaustion, when my courage had almost gone, I determined to take my problem to God. My head in my hands, I bowed over the kitchen table and prayed aloud. The words I spoke to God that midnight are still vivid in my memory. "I am here taking a stand for what I believe is right. But now I am afraid. The people are looking to me for leadership, and if I stand before them without strength and courage, they too will falter. I am at the end of my powers. I have nothing left. I've come to the point where I can't face it alone."

At that moment I experienced the presence of the Divine as I had never before experienced him. It seemed as though I could hear the quiet assurance of an inner voice, saying, "Stand up for righteousness, stand up for truth. God will be at your side forever." I was ready to face anything. The outer situation remained the same, but God had given me inner calm.[1]

Our fears and longings are significant; our doubts are real. Yet we can speak, for just as God was with Martin Luther King, Jr., God is with us as we stand up in our relationships, our workplaces, and our communities.

Nearly every day we can find frustrations that result from someone's reluctance to speak. There is no reason to hold our breath. When we swim, our giving and receiving breaths enable us to move through the water. Speaking and listening generously help propel us through difficult situations. When we speak our stands clearly, our personal relationships become vital and fresh.

Notes

Publishing information not given here appears at the end under Suggested Reading.

Chapter 2: When You Are Afraid of Conflict

1. Stephen Neill, *Christian Holiness* (New York: Harper & Brothers, 1960), p. 72.
2. Jean Baker Miller, *Toward a New Psychology of Women,* pp. 17, 126.
3. Walter Kempler, *Principles of Gestalt Family Therapy* (Costa Mesa, Calif.: Kempler Institute, 1974), pp. 67–68.
4. Carl Rogers, *Becoming Partners: Marriage and Its Alternatives* (New York: Dell Publishing Co., 1972), p. 24.

Chapter 3: When You Are Not Sure Where You Stand

1. Meg Gerrard, "Emotional and Cognitive Barriers to Effective Contraception: Are Males and Females Really Different?" in Kathryn Kelley, ed., *Females, Males, and Sexuality* (Albany, N.Y.: State University of New York Press, 1987), pp. 222–223.
2. Ibid., p. 237.
3. Ibid., pp. 218–220.

Chapter 4: When You Don't Think You Have Enough Power

1. Jean Baker Miller, *Toward a New Psychology of Women,* p. 116.

2. Mary Field Belenky et al., *Women's Ways of Knowing,* p. 30.

3. Eleanor Emmons Maccoby and Carol Nagy Jacklin, *The Psychology of Sex Differences* (Stanford, Calif.: Stanford University Press, 1974), p. 351, and Belenky et al., *Women's Ways,* p. 5.

4. Belenky et al., *Women's Ways,* p. 84.

5. Nelle Morton, *The Journey Is Home,* especially pp. 60, 73, 82, and 129.

6. Molly Young Brown, *The Unfolding Self.* This resource contains over a dozen exercises that are helpful in strengthening the will and in mobilizing internal resources. Another useful book with similar exercises is Piero Ferrucci, *What We May Be: Techniques for Psychological and Spiritual Growth Through Psychosynthesis.*

7. Brown, *The Unfolding Self,* pp. 69–70.

Chapter 5: When and How to Speak

1. One place where Carl Rogers uses the term "persisting feelings" is in his book *Becoming Partners: Marriage and Its Alternatives* (New York: Dell Publishing Co., 1972), p. 203.

2. Jacqueline Haessly, *Peacemaking: Family Activities for Justice and Peace,* p. 49.

Chapter 6: Empowering Others to Speak

1. Robert Coles, *Women of Crisis: Lives of Struggle and Hope* (New York: Dell Publishing Co., 1978), pp. 19–20.

2. Nelle Morton, *The Journey Is Home,* p. 205.

3. E. H. Porter, *An Introduction to Therapeutic Counseling* (Boston: Houghton Mifflin Co., 1950).

4. A variety of books explains active listening techniques. I recommend (even for people who are not preparing for marriage) Joan Hunt and Richard Hunt, *Preparing for Christian Marriage,* pp. 28–35.

5. *King Lear,* V.III.325–326.

Chapter 7: Giving and Receiving Speech

1. Martin Luther King, Jr., *Strength to Love* (Philadelphia: Fortress Press, 1981), pp. 113–114.

Suggested Reading

Belenky, Mary Field, et al. *Women's Ways of Knowing: The Development of Self, Voice, and Mind.* New York: Basic Books, 1986.

Brown, Molly Young. *The Unfolding Self: Psychosynthesis and Counseling.* Los Angeles: Psychosynthesis Press, 1983.

Dorn, Lois. *Peace in the Family: A Workbook of Ideas and Actions.* New York: Pantheon Books, 1983.

Ferrucci, Piero. *What We May Be: Techniques for Psychological and Spiritual Growth.* Los Angeles: J. P. Tarcher, 1982.

Haessly, Jacqueline. *Peacemaking: Family Activities for Justice and Peace.* New York: Paulist Press, 1980.

Hulme, William E. *Mind Your Tongue: Communication in the Family.* Philadelphia: Westminster Press, 1988.

Hunt, Joan, and Richard Hunt. *Preparing for Christian Marriage.* Nashville: Abingdon Press, 1982.

Miller, Jean Baker. *Toward a New Psychology of Women,* 2nd ed. Boston: Beacon Press, 1986.

Morton, Nelle. *The Journey Is Home.* Boston: Beacon Press, 1985.

Robbins, Joan H., and Rachel J. Siegel, eds. *Women Changing Therapy.* New York: Harrington Park Press, 1985.

Seifert, Harvey. *What on Earth? Making Personal Decisions on Controversial Issues.* Washington, D.C.: General Board of Church and Society of the United Methodist Church, 1986.

Swartley, Willard. *Slavery, Sabbath, and Women: Case Issues in Biblical Interpretation.* Scottdale, Pa.: Herald Press, 1983.

Taylor, Jeremy. *Dream Work: Techniques for Discovering the Creative Power of Dreams.* New York: Paulist Press, 1983.